Weapons and Warfare

Don Nardo
AR B.L.: 10.8 Alt.: 1585
Points: 6.0

UG

WORLD
HISTORY SERIES

Weapons and Warfare

by
Don Nardo

LUCENT
BOOKS®

THOMSON

GALE

San Diego • Detroit • New York • San Francisco • Cleveland • New Haven, Conn. • Waterville, Maine • London • Munich

LIBRARY OF CONGRESS CATALOGING-IN-PUBLICATION DATA

Nardo, Don, 1947–
   History of weapons and warfare / by Don Nardo.
     p. cm. — (World history series)
Includes bibliographical references and index.
Contents: Stone Age warfare and the Native Americans—Military innovations in the ancient
Near East—Greece and Rome at war: the rise of the West—Knights and castles in medieval
Europe and Japan—The fast, fierce armies of the Asian conquerors—Musket and bayonet:
linear warfare emerges—Industrializing the battlefield: the first modern wars—Crushing
ordeal of total warfare: World War II.
   ISBN 1-59018-183-2 (hardback : alk. paper)
   1. Military weapons—History—Juvenile literature. [1. Military weapons—History.]
2. War—History.] I. Title. II. Series.
   U804.A1N37 2004
   355.8'2'09—dc22
                                       2003019408

Contents

Foreword

Each year on the first day of school, nearly every history teacher faces the task of explaining why his or her students should study history. One logical answer to this question is that exploring what happened in our past explains how the things we often take for granted—our customs, ideas, and institutions—came to be. As statesman and historian Winston Churchill put it, "Every nation or group of nations has its own tale to tell. Knowledge of the trials and struggles is necessary to all who would comprehend the problems, perils, challenges, and opportunities which confront us today." Thus, a study of history puts modern ideas and institutions in perspective. For example, though the founders of the United States were talented and creative thinkers, they clearly did not invent the concept of democracy. Instead, they adapted some democratic ideas that had originated in ancient Greece and with which the Romans, the British, and others had experimented. An exploration of these cultures, then, reveals their very real connection to us through institutions that continue to shape our daily lives.

Another reason often given for studying history is the idea that lessons exist in the past from which contemporary societies can benefit and learn. This idea, although controversial, has always been an intriguing one for historians. Those who agree that society can benefit from the past often quote philosopher George Santayana's famous statement, "Those who cannot remember the past are condemned to repeat it." Historians who subscribe to Santayana's philosophy believe that, for example, studying the events that led up to the major world wars or other significant historical events would allow society to chart a different and more favorable course in the future.

Just as difficult as convincing students of the importance of studying history is the search for useful and interesting supplementary materials that present historical events in a context that can be easily understood. The volumes in Lucent Books' World History Series attempt to present a broad, balanced, and penetrating view of the march of history. Ancient Egypt's important wars and rulers, for example, are presented against the rich and colorful backdrop of Egyptian religious, social, and cultural developments. The series engages the reader by enhancing historical events with these cultural contexts. For example, in *Ancient Greece*, the text covers the role of women in that society. Slavery is discussed in *The Roman Empire*, as well as how slaves earned their freedom. The numerous and varied aspects of everyday life in these and other societies are explored in each volume of the series. Additionally, the series covers the major political, cultural, and philosophical ideas as the torch of civilization is passed from ancient Mesopotamia and Egypt, through Greece, Rome, Medieval Europe, and other world cultures, to the modern day.

The material in the series is formatted in a thorough, precise, and organized manner. Each volume offers the reader a comprehensive and clearly written overview of an important historical event or period. The topic under discussion is placed in a broad, historical context. For example, *The Italian Renaissance* begins with a discussion of the High Middle Ages and the loss of central control that allowed certain Italian cities to develop artistically. The book ends by looking forward to the Reformation and interpreting the societal changes that grew out of the Renaissance. Thus, students are not only involved in an historical era, but also enveloped by the events leading up to that era and the events following it.

One important and unique feature in the World History Series is the primary and secondary source quotations that richly supplement each volume. These quotes are useful in a number of ways. First, they allow students access to sources they would not normally be exposed to because of the difficulty and obscurity of the original source. The quotations range from interesting anecdotes to farsighted cultural perspectives and are drawn from historical witnesses both past and present. Second, the quotes demonstrate how and where historians themselves derive their information on the past as they strive to reach a consensus on historical events. Lastly, all of the quotes are footnoted, familiarizing students with the citation process and allowing them to verify quotes and/or look up the original source if the quote piques their interest.

Finally, the books in the World History Series provide a detailed launching point for further research. Each book contains a bibliography specifically geared toward student research. A second, annotated bibliography introduces students to all the sources the author consulted when compiling the book. A chronology of important dates gives students an overview, at a glance, of the topic covered. Where applicable, a glossary of terms is included.

In short, the series is designed not only to acquaint readers with the basics of history, but also to make them aware that their lives are a part of an ongoing human saga. Perhaps then they will come to the same realization as famed historian Arnold Toynbee. In his monumental work, *A Study of History*, he wrote about becoming aware of history flowing through him in a mighty current, and of his own life "welling like a wave in the flow of this vast tide."

IMPORTANT DATES IN THE HISTORY OF WEAPONS AND WARFARE

ca. 12,000
The bow and arrow is invented.

ca. 1274
The Egyptians and Hittites clash at Kadesh in history's first battle recorded in any detail.

334
Macedonian Greek conqueror Alexander the Great invades the Persian Empire.

ca. 370
The Huns sweep into eastern Europe, driving other peoples into Rome's northern provinces.

1494
French king Charles VIII shocks Europe by using cannons to demolish several Italian castles.

ca. 1690–1700
Flintlock muskets begin to be manufactured in quantity.

ca. 12,000 B.C.–197 B.C.	200 A.D.	600	1000	1400	1800

197
The Romans decisively defeat the Greeks at Cynoscephalae, in central Greece.

490
The Greeks defeat an invading force of Persians at Marathon, signaling the rise of the West.

ca. 4000–3000
Metal weapons begin to appear in the Near East.

ca. 8000–7000
Towns fortified by defensive walls begin to rise in the Near East.

1784
An English artilleryman invents shrapnel.

1346
English longbowmen defeat French knights at Crécy, during the Hundred Years' War.

ca. 1280
The Mongol Empire, created by Genghis Khan, reaches its greatest extent.

634
A series of Arab conquests of the Near East and North Africa begins.

1815
After advancing the art of warfare, French dictator Napoleon Bonaparte is defeated at Waterloo.

1861–1865
The American Civil War, which many experts see as the first modern war, occurs.

1939
German dictator Adolf Hitler invades Poland, igniting World War II.

1941
The Japanese bomb the American naval base at Pearl Harbor, bringing the United States into the war.

2003
The United States attacks Iraq and deposes the regime of widely hated dictator Saddam Hussein.

1810	1840	1870	1900	1930	1960	1990

1914–1918
Europe is ravaged by World War I, which introduces tanks and airplanes to warfare.

1945
Germany surrenders to the Allies. The United States drops atomic bombs on Japan, which also surrenders.

1991
An international coalition led by the United States attacks Iraq and liberates Kuwait, which the Iraqis had captured.

2001
On September 11, Islamic terrorists fly airplanes into New York's World Trade Center towers, killing three thousand people.

The Most Theatrical of Human Activities

Like it or not, war is an inevitable part of the human condition. Untold thousands of conflicts, big and small, have raged across the globe since the first written records appeared. And historians believe that wars were common long before humans learned to write. Moreover, hundreds of millions of men, women, and children lost their lives in these conflicts. More than 45 million people perished in the six years of World War II alone. And it is likely that millions more will die in the centuries to come.

WRONG AND RIGHT REASONS FOR WAR

The reasons for going to war have varied widely. Settling political, social, and/or religious disputes was a frequent motivation for fighting, as was the desire to acquire the territory, resources, or possessions of others. Hatred, fear, and revenge were other common causes of conflict. All of these motives for war were and remain, to one degree or another, reckless, selfish, exploitive, and based on the least worthy of human emotions and reactions. The great American mil-

itary historian Victor Davis Hanson calls them "soulless." The pages of history, he says, are filled with examples of famous generals leading their troops to victory for the wrong reasons:

> Alexander, Hannibal, Caesar, Napoleon, and other great marshals used their tactical and strategic genius to alter history through the brutality of their armies. None led democratic soldiers. They freed no slaves nor liberated the oppressed. They were all aggressors, who created their matchless forces to kill rather than to preserve.... None were great men, and praise of their military prowess is forever tainted by the evil they wrought and the innocent they killed. They and their armies were without a moral sense and purpose, and thus their battles, tactically brilliant though they were, were soulless.[1]

In contrast, at least a few wars have been fought for the *right* reasons. In fourth-century B.C. Greece, for instance, Epaminondas, the great Theban general, broke the back of the Spartan army, which had long struck fear into the hearts of Greeks everywhere. After defeating the Spartans in open battle, Epaminondas freed the 200,000 serfs Sparta had held in abject bondage for generations. Freedom and self-rule were also the goals of the American patriots who challenged Britain in 1776. And the commitment of the Allies in World War II to stop the German and Japanese militarists from enslaving humanity was both justified and moral. "Only when free men march . . . toward the heartland of their enemy in hopes of saving the doomed," says Hanson,

> when their vast armies are aimed at salvation and liberation, not conquest and enslavement . . . does battle take on a spiritual dimension, one that defines a culture, teaches it what civic militarism is and how it is properly used.[2]

FASCINATION ALONG WITH HORROR

Whatever the reasons for and moral dimensions of war might be, armed conflict remains a bloody business in which nations often rise and fall and innocent civilians are killed or maimed along with the soldiers. Indeed, war has consistently shaped and reshaped societies and the personal lives of the people within them. Perhaps no other human endeavor is as spectacular, sensational, influential, destructive, feared, and held in awe as war is. For this reason, throughout history soldiers and civilians alike have reacted with larger-than-life emotions and actions and

This scene from Stanley Kubrick's 2001: A Space Odyssey *captures the discovery of the first weapon by humanity's forebears.*

displayed their best and worst qualities during wartime. In the words of Illinois scholar Lawrence H. Keeley:

> Warfare concentrates and intensifies some of our strongest emotions: courage and fear, resignation and panic, selfishness and self-sacrifice, greed and generosity, patriotism and xenophobia [fear of foreigners]. The stimulus of war has incited human beings to . . . ingenuity, improvisation, cooperation, vandalism, and cruelty. It is the riskiest field on which to match wits and luck. No peaceful endeavor can equal its penalties for failure, and few can exceed its rewards for success. It remains the most theatrical of human activities, combining tragedy, high drama[,] . . . spectacle, action, farce, and even low comedy. War displays the human condition in extremes.[3]

One notable side effect of the sheer spectacle of war is that the events and methods of warfare inevitably fascinate people as much as they horrify them. This explains the present high level of interest in warfare and the weapons, generals, strategies, tactics, and casualties associated with it. "Why is reflection on warfare . . . generating such interest today?" asks military historian John Hackett. He answers:

> Fear of war is felt in these times everywhere, fueled by the conviction that modern technology has brought us to a point where the unlimited use by great powers of the weapons of war now available . . . could threaten the survival of humanity. Another notable feature of the world we live in is a great and growing interest in the past. . . . An inevitable result of the convergence of . . . fear of war and interest in the past has been a thirst for more information about the making of war in earlier times, not only in terms of tools [and] techniques . . . used in warfare, but also of the people by whom wars are and have been fought.[4]

Studies of the history of warfare therefore provide a wealth of information about human societies, both past and present. All have been shaped by war to one degree or another. And learning how this has happened can help people achieve a better understanding of their roots, their world, themselves, and, just maybe, how future wars might be prevented.

1 Stone Age Warfare and the Native Americans

Modern scholars do not and may never know when the first war took place. The identity and particulars of that milestone in human development are likely forever lost in the mists of the dim past. Of course, the search for the earliest examples of warfare is partly determined by one's definition of war. There is little doubt that even the most primitive human ancestors engaged in one-on-one fights from time to time. Periodic physical contests over territory, mating rights, and food have been observed in nearly all mammal species, including humanity's nearest relatives, chimpanzees.

But can such individualized aggressive behavior, most of it driven by instinct, be classified as war? The experts agree that it cannot. True warfare, they say, involves deliberate planning, organization, and coordinated attacks. Evidence suggests that such attacks, likely using sticks and stones as weapons, first took place sometime in what scholars call the Paleolithic Age, or "Old Stone Age"; this was the period of human history that began with the appearance of the first stone tools, perhaps 2 million or more years ago.

By the advent of the Neolithic Age, more lethal weapons, such as the bow and arrow, had appeared. (Neolithic means "New Stone Age." The period dates from about 10,000 B.C., when agriculture began, to roughly 3000 B.C., when people began making metal tools and weapons.) These weapons, along with more organized and complex tactics, made warfare larger in scale and more deadly.

Modern scholars obviously cannot go back in time to study Paleolithic and Neolithic

These artifacts from the Paleolithic Age include primitive arrowheads and spearheads.

fighters firsthand. But they can observe the behaviors of the few cultures left on Earth that still use Stone Age tools and weapons. Up until European whites invaded their lands and altered their lifestyles, the Native Americans were among the last remaining Neolithic cultures. In the nineteenth and twentieth centuries, the traditional customs of the North and South American Indians were intensely studied and documented. These studies reveal much about the weapons and tactics of Neolithic warfare.

FROM HUNTING TO RAIDING

In their quest for the very origins of warfare, however, scholars must go back to a time long before the first Native Americans migrated to the Americas (perhaps between 50,000 and 40,000 B.C.). Indeed, if warfare is defined as consciously planned, organized violence, the first examples probably took place hundreds of thousands of years ago. Scholars more or less unanimously agree that the first planned, loosely organized violence was hunting related. "There is considerable evidence," noted historian Arther Ferrill points out, "that organized groups of men, almost certainly under the command of a leader, helped to stampede large animals over cliffs or to draw them into bogs."[5]

Sometime during the Paleolithic Age, one or more bands or tribes of humans began to apply the methods of these planned, cooperative hunts to attacks on other groups of

A reconstructed scene of primitive human hunters attacking a mammoth trapped in a bog. Scholars believe that weapons were first used for hunting.

EARLY SHOCK WEAPONS

In this excerpt from his book War Before Civilization, *Lawrence H. Keeley explains why during the Stone Age "shock" weapons such as clubs often did more serious damage than missile weapons like arrows.*

"The heavier weight of shock weapons . . . [imparts] a greater force at impact than that generated by necessarily lighter missiles. Once a missile is released, it is unguided, whereas a shock weapon's path can be adjusted to track the target. A single blow from such weapons can severely wound or kill outright an unarmored opponent. It is no surprise, then, to read of skulls being crushed, brains dashed out, limbs fractured or severed, and torsos pierced through by such weapons. For example, an Aztec warrior could decapitate a Spanish horse with a single blow of his obsidian-edged sword-club."

people. Such tribal raids can be thought of as a primitive form of warfare. The desire to acquire another tribe's cave, territory, or food may have been a driving force behind these attacks. Studies of North American Indian tribes show that another common motivation was revenge. Many of these tribes called it "mourning" warfare. According to Cherokee historian Tom Holm, this was a highly ritualized form of blood vengeance based on deep feelings of spirituality:

> When a kinsman or kinswoman died or was killed in battle, some groups believed, the clan's, tribe's, or nation's collective spiritual power was diminished directly in proportion to that of the slain person. Retaliatory raiding took place to take captives and/or kill a certain number of enemy warriors. In numerous cases, captives were adopted as replacements for deceased relatives. Killing an enemy or torturing a captive to death was intended to repair the metaphysical imbalance caused by a

death. Some native American women literally "dried their tears" with the scalps of enemies killed in battle. [6]

Raids on rival tribes must have been frequent during the Paleolithic and Neolithic eras. Among the tribes of the American West, between 80 and 90 percent engaged in warfare involving raids at least once a year. And many villages were raided at least twice a year. One primitive South American village observed by scholars was raided twenty-five times in fifteen months. Most such raids killed only a few people at a time. Occasionally, however, they became massacres intended to annihilate an enemy. "In one case of [a primitive tribal] massacre in New Guinea," Lawrence Keeley writes,

> the victim group of 300 lost about 8 percent of its population. In a case from a different area, a tribal confederation of 1,000 people lost nearly 13 percent of its population in just the first hour of an attack. [7]

Although periodic, small-scale raids and massacres likely constituted the earliest and most primitive forms of warfare, they were not large, organized, and sophisticated enough from a military standpoint to be called actual wars. Once the signal to begin a raid had been given, for instance, individual attackers probably acted on their own, without much coordination as a unit. So these events cannot be thought of as *organized* warfare. As Ferrill puts it:

> At the risk of grotesque simplification, let me suggest that "organized warfare" can best be defined with one word. The word is *formation*. . . . When warriors are put into the field in formation, when they work as a team under a commander or leader rather than as a band of leaderless heroes, they have crossed the line (it has been called "the military horizon") from "primitive" to "true" or "organized" warfare.[8]

INTRODUCTION OF MORE LETHAL WEAPONS

Part of the reason that warfare lacked formations and remained primitive for so long was the nature of the weapons used. Throughout most of Paleolithic times, weapons were limited to wooden clubs, rocks, and simple spears. All early peoples used such weapons, so all were more or less evenly matched. Modes of fighting, therefore, tended to remain static for long periods of time.

Toward the end of the Paleolithic Age, however, several considerably more sophisticated and deadly weapons appeared. The first was the atlatl, dating from perhaps 25,000 B.C. Eventually used by hunter-gatherers across the globe, it was essentially a throwing stick about eighteen inches long with a wooden handle connected to a wooden socket or groove in the rear. The

This model of an atlatl shows how the operator controlled the weapon with the thumb and index finger. An atlatl could fire a projectile several hundred feet.

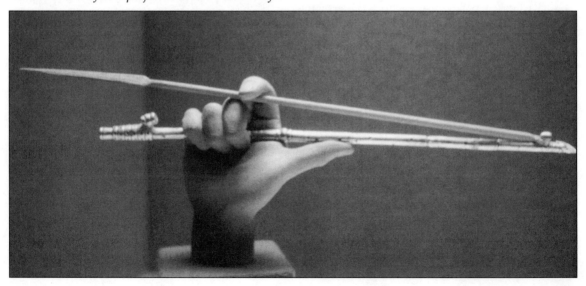

user inserted a short spear or dart into the socket and fired the projectile by snapping the stick with a forceful overhand motion. This gave the spear much more forward momentum than was possible by simply using one's arm. The first versions of the atlatl may have appeared in northwest Africa. European tribes had them at least seventeen thousand years ago, and, as scholar Grant Keddie points out:

> Immigrants from Siberia likely brought the atlatl to North America, where it was used to hunt large animals by at least 10,000–12,000 years ago. . . . The Inuit and Aleut of the Arctic, the Tlingit peoples of the southern coast of Alaska and northern coast of British Columbia, and some peoples of southeastern United States, Mexico and northern South America, still used the atlatl when Europeans first arrived.[9]

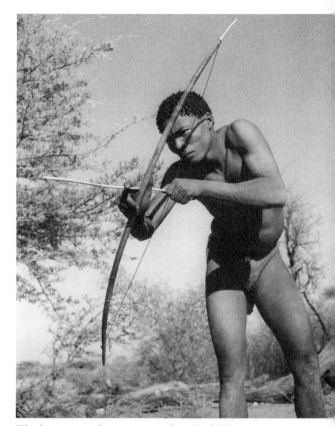

The bow proved superior to the atlatl. This African hunter prepares to shoot a poisoned arrow at his prey.

THE BOW

Several thousand years after the introduction of the atlatl, around 12,000 B.C., an even more deadly weapon—the bow and arrow (usually referred to simply as the bow)—appeared. The bow had more propulsive power than either a throwing spear or atlatl, as well as other advantages. According to Ferrill:

> The spear, when used as a throwing weapon . . . had a range of about fifty yards. The bow . . . doubled that. Moreover, it was an inexpensive weapon—at least the simple bow of the Neolithic Age was. Anyone could make one and kill from a concealed position at a distance. When a group of people acted together and fired on command, they could unleash a mighty barrage of fire, and a single warrior could carry far more arrows than spears.[10]

Because the bow allowed a person to kill "at a distance," the user did not need to fight hand to hand with an enemy. Inevitably, the best marksmen stopped being all-around fighters and began doing nothing else but firing arrow after arrow. The emergence of such expert archers likely marked the beginning of specialization in weapons training and use. Another new long-range weapon, the sling, also fell into the hands of specialists, who, with enough practice, could achieve lethal results. As Ferrill says, "A heavy, fist-sized stone slung from the sling can smash skulls or break arms, ribs, and legs."[11]

BLADED WEAPONS

Another new weapon, the stone dagger, was a larger, more dangerous form of the stone cutting tools that primitive humans had been making for close to 2 million years. Sophisticated stone daggers have been found at Neolithic sites in the Near East dating to 7000 B.C., so the first versions almost certainly appeared several thousands of years earlier. A number of finely made specimens have also been found in early Native American sites. What made these weapons so effective was the extreme sharpness of their blades. To achieve this sharpness, artisans chipped and beveled pieces of relatively soft stone in a process called flaking. Colin F. Taylor, an authority on Native American weapons, explains the process as it occurred in North America:

> The natural edges or forms of the stone were modified by fracturing with a specially made flaking tool. The "flaker," as it was commonly called, had a blade generally of antler [deer or elk horn], ivory, or hard bone, set in a wooden handle. This was applied to the stone edge and, with a quick movement (at the same time exerting a strong pressure), a flake of the stone was forced off.

> A skilled individual worked rapidly, moving along the outline of the blade, producing a razor-sharp, although fragile, cutting edge.[12]

Such methods of flaking stone to produce sharp edges also contributed to advances in club making. Old-style wooden clubs or versions with rounded lumps of stone tied to wooden handles gave way to clubs whose heads had sharper edges, and to stone axes.

EARLY BATTLE FORMATIONS

How did such advances in weaponry lead to more organized and advanced forms of warfare? To begin with, those tribes that lacked the newest weapon (whatever it might be) were at a distinct disadvantage. However, they eventually managed to acquire the weapon themselves. But soon, a neighboring group would begin using one or more other weapons, necessitating the nearby tribes without them to do their best to catch up and achieve parity. In this way, military technology began to progress more rapidly.

Even when two sides were evenly matched in new weaponry, one way to achieve the advantage was by using these weapons in more organized and devastating ways; this naturally led to the steady invention of various battlefield formations and tactics. Evidence for such formations and tactics in early Neolithic times comes in the form of primitive cave paintings found in Spain. One painting shows a group of warriors carrying bows and marching in unison in a line. Lines and columns of fight-

This Stone Age painting found on the wall of a cave in Spain shows a primitive battle scene in which tribesmen use spears and other weapons.

ers are the most basic of all battle formations. The figure at the head of the line wears a distinctive headdress, suggesting he is the leader, perhaps a Stone Age version of a military general.

Another painting found in Spain shows archers firing in unison on command. And still another depicts an actual battle in which the warriors in one group are trying to outflank their opponents. (In military terms, the flanks are the sides of a troop formation; a flanking maneuver is one in which soldiers attempt to fire on or attack the flanks and rear of the enemy formation.) Only seven fighters are shown in this rendering. Yet surely they are meant to represent larger numbers. It is perfectly credible that a large tribe living in Europe, the Near East, or North America in 10,000 B.C. could have fielded an army of a hundred or even a thousand or more warriors.

ADVANCES IN DEFENSIVE MEASURES

With the introduction of more effective and deadly weapons and tactics, one would expect to see the development of better defensive measures to counter them. And this is exactly what the evidence shows. About 8000 B.C., defensive walls, some enclosing small towns, began to appear across the eastern Mediterranean and Near East. The earliest and perhaps best-known example is Jericho, in the Jordan valley in Palestine. The original defensive wall was ten feet thick and thirteen feet high, and enclosed an area of almost eleven acres. "The population of Jericho at this stage was probably around 2,000," Ferrill points out. "If there were 500 to 600 fighting men, it would have been possible to station one defender for every yard of the wall."[13]

A larger fortified town, which covered perhaps thirty-two acres, rose in the seventh millennium (the 6000s) B.C. at Catal Huyuk in southeastern Asia Minor (present-day Turkey). According to archaeologist Trevor Watkins:

> The town's square, flat-roofed houses were built side by side like a pile of children's building blocks, pushed together. Access to each house was by means of a door at roof-level, from which a steep ladder led down into the living area. Circulation [movement] around the settlement was across the flat roofs. The edge of such a settlement would have presented a solid, blank wall to any intruder or attacker. Once the ladders . . . were drawn up, the settlement would have been impregnable.[14]

Another defensive measure that developed in Neolithic times was primitive body armor. Made of materials like animal hide and wood, remnants of such armor have been found in the Near East and the Americas. Warriors of the Tlingit tribe, for example, wore a wooden cuirass (chest protector). The front section was made of ten vertical wooden slats bound together with strips of animal sinew (tendon) and rawhide. Attached to the end slats were sections made of lightweight, somewhat flexible wooden rods, also placed vertically. Wide rawhide strips attached to the top-front of the armor ran back over the wearer's shoulder and connected to the back section, which was composed of slats just like the front.

The Tlingit, along with several other Native American tribes, including the Shoshone, Pawnee, Navajo, and Mohawk, also used cuirasses made from hide. Such armor usually consisted of two or more layers of leather stitched together with rawhide

CHOOSING TO HIDE RATHER THAN FIGHT

In contrast with the vast majority of Native American tribes, the Shoshone did not engage in warfare before the appearance of white Europeans. Peter Farb explains why in this tract from his acclaimed book about the rise of Indian cultures.

"The explanation lies not in some superior Shoshone ethic . . . but in more practical matters. The Shoshone did not wage war because they had no reason to. They had no desire to gain military honors, for these were meaningless in their kind of society [a very simple one based completely on mutual cooperation]. They had no territories to defend, for a territory is valuable only at those times when it is producing food, and those were precisely the times when the Shoshone cooperated, rather than made war. Even if they had wanted to steal from richer neighboring Indians, they lacked both the weapons and a society sufficiently complex to be organized for concerted action. Whenever other Indians invaded their lands and attacked them, Shoshone did not fight back but simply ran away and hid."

strips. Elk was perhaps the most common type of hide employed, but moose, buffalo, and other large mammals were also exploited. The fronts of such cuirasses were usually elaborately decorated.

GRUESOME EVIDENCE FROM GRAVE SITES

Proof that both offensive and defensive modes of warfare had become common and very brutal by late Paleolithic and early Neolithic times comes from studies of skeletons found in ancient grave sites. Burials dating to the period of 34,000–22,000 B.C. in central and western Europe included many people who were killed by weapons. A skeleton found in Italy has a point from a spear or atlatl imbedded in the spine; a skull found in France shows evidence of scalping; and numerous skulls of adult males have fractures caused by clubs.

Particularly telling is the gruesome evidence from a cemetery located near the border between Egypt and Sudan, used between 12,000 and 5000 B.C. Of the fifty-nine skeletons found there, more than 40 percent have stone projectiles lodged in them. One body was pierced six times, another nineteen times, and a third twenty-one times. In addition, it appears that some of these unfortunate individuals were shot through the mouth with arrows while they were lying on their backs, which suggests that they had already fallen in battle and were systematically finished off by enemy troops. "Overkill may be a modern concept," Ferrill remarks, "but it was an ancient practice."[15]

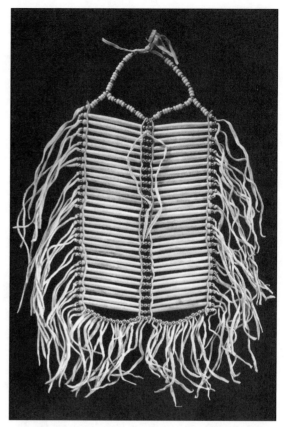

This style of cuirass, used by some Native American plains tribes, is made of many tough rawhide strips.

Similar burial sites with skeletons bearing war wounds have been found in Germany, France, North Africa, and the American West. The evidence shows clearly that warfare is not a recent development. Untold thousands of wars were fought long before the first one recorded in any detail (a little more than three thousand years ago). The causes, events, and outcomes of those conflicts, which were surely momentous to the participants, have long since vanished forever. This is a potent reminder that time remains a far greater conqueror than any human army.

Chapter

2 Military Innovations in the Ancient Near East

The next great military innovation after the introduction of the bow in late Paleolithic times and stone defensive walls in the Neolithic Age was the ability to smelt and make weapons of metal. Copper was the first metal people learned to separate from rocks. And soon they began combining it with small amounts of tin to produce an alloy called bronze, which is considerably stronger and more durable than copper. (At first, bronze was not as plentiful as copper because tin was scarce. Over time, supplies of tin were distributed through trade.)

The advent of the Bronze Age occurred at different times in different places. It happened first on a large scale in the Near East in the fourth millennium (the 3000s) B.C., and, not surprisingly, the new technology transformed the face of warfare in that area. "The beginnings of the Bronze Age are roughly contemporary with the appearance of civilization in the Near East," Arther Ferrill writes, "and one of the main features of the new period, metal weapons, made warfare a much more lethal activity than it had been in Neolithic times." [16]

The "civilization" Ferrill speaks of consisted of the rise of the first cities, large-scale stone architecture, and written records in Sumeria, the fertile region lying northwest of the Persian Gulf. The larger surrounding area, centered on the Tigris and Euphrates Rivers, became known as Mesopotamia (the "land between the rivers"). And the Sumerians and later peoples who followed them in the region—including the Babylonians and Assyrians—all of whom shared similar social customs and military practices, are collectively called Mesopotamians.

The ability to make metal weapons was not the only important military development in early Mesopotamia. Many of the first cities rapidly grew to have populations in the tens of thousands. This allowed for amassing the largest armies yet seen in the world—some having up to ten thousand or more soldiers. In the hands of a few talented and ambitious men, such powerful forces were used for wholesale conquest and the creation of the world's first empires.

Under these conditions, most major new military innovations in the fourth, third, and second millennia B.C. originated in Mesopotamia. (A few filtered into that region from central Asia and were improved on and applied on a larger scale by the Mesopotamians.) Over time, these innovations steadily spread outward to Palestine, Egypt, Asia Minor, and other parts of the Near East, and eventually to eastern Europe.

Early Near Eastern Weapons

The first major military development in the Near East—the transition from stone to metal weapons—did not occur all at once. Even after the introduction of metal-smelting techniques, Stone Age versions of some weapons, particularly clubs, or maces, remained in use for a number of centuries. Over time, stone knife and ax blades, spearheads, arrowheads, and so on were replaced by versions made of copper, bronze, and eventually iron.

The rate at which this transition took place and the quality of the weapons produced depended on how effective the metalworking techniques were in a given region and era. The development of metal swords is a case in point. In early fourth-millennium B.C. Mesopotamia and as late as the third millennium B.C. in Egypt, swords had serious limitations. In these places and times, copper was the only metal widely used for weapons. The problem was that copper is a relatively soft metal, which means that a long copper blade swung in a slashing or hacking motion can easily break. (Such a blade also did not keep its edge very long.) As a result, at first swords were secondary backup weapons used only occasionally in battle.

At left are two bronze ax-heads; at right, bronze swords. Bronze, a mixture of copper and tin, proved harder and more durable than copper alone.

The primary early Near Eastern weapons remained maces, axes, spears, and bows. Many of the maces had stone heads made of the hardest kinds of rock available in a given region. Over time, some military organizations switched to copper mace heads. For fighting at close quarters, the mace was used to break skulls and other bones, but soldiers also needed a weapon with a large blade that could chop off an enemy's hand or leg or slice through enemy shields. (Many soldiers now carried shields, usually made of wooden frames covered by animal hide.) Early sword blades were not only too soft but also too thin for the job. The battle-ax, in contrast, had a much wider and therefore stronger blade, even when it was made of copper. Metal battle-axes were employed all across the Near East for at least three thousand years.

Of the early Near Eastern missile weapons, the metal-tipped throwing spear, or javelin, was in use throughout the region by the end of the fourth millennium B.C. It consisted of a long wooden staff topped by a leaf-shaped blade of copper or bronze that was tied to the shaft by cords. Another early Near Eastern missile weapon—the bow—was not much different from Neolithic versions. The most common type, called the "self" or "simple" bow, had a wooden shaft, ranging from three-and-a-half to seven feet in length, that was strung with a cord made of tightly twisted animal gut. The only major innovation in the weapon during this period was the transition from stone- to metal-tipped arrowheads. For the moment, therefore, the bow remained the least revolutionary weapon in the region and did only minimal damage to enemies protected by shields.

EARLY BATTLEFIELD UNITS, FORMATIONS, AND TACTICS

Naturally, the effectiveness of any of these early weapons depended to a considerable degree on how they were used in large battlefield formations. When two opposing armies were armed with the same weapons, the one with the most soldiers and the superior battle plan and tactics had a clear advantage. But to put large numbers of armed fighters in the field at one time was (and remains even today) an expensive and difficult undertaking. Early commanders learned that they could reduce confusion, disorder, and cost, and at the same time increase speed and efficiency by organizing their armies into manageable units of varying sizes.

The Assyrians, for example, had a very effective breakdown of army units by the late second millennium B.C. It was likely based to some degree on that of earlier Mesopotamian peoples, including the Sumerians. The king was the army's commander in chief, while his assistant, or "field marshal," was in charge of moving the army from place to place and preparing it for battle. Under the field marshal were lesser officers, each in command of a unit of troops. The units were composed of 1,000, 200, 100, 50, and 10 men each. So, for each commander of 1,000, there were five subcommanders of 200, ten of 100, twenty of 50, and a hundred of 10.

The army units of Egypt in the second millennium B.C. broke down in a fairly similar manner. According to Ferrill:

> The pharaoh often served as commander-in-chief . . . although other generals were occasionally in command of in-

NEAR EASTERN WARRIORS FIGHT TO THE DEATH

This contemporary account of an ancient Egyptian engaging a Syrian in single combat with bows, battle-axes, and javelins comes from the famous story of the Egyptian courtier Sinuhe (quoted in James B. Pritchard's Ancient Near Eastern Texts Relating to the Old Testament*).*

"A mighty man of Retenu [Syria] came, that he might challenge me in my own camp. He was a hero without peer, and he had [beaten all opponents in his land]. . . . During the night I strung my bow and shot my arrows [in a practice session] . . . and I polished my weapons. When day broke . . . he came to me as I was waiting. . . . Every heart burned for me; women and men groaned. . . . Then he took his shield and his battleax and his armful of javelins. Now after I had let his weapons issue forth [without doing me any damage] . . . he charged me and I shot him, my arrow sticking in his neck. He cried out and fell on his nose. I [finished him off] with his own battleax and raised my cry of victory . . . while every Asiatic roared. . . . Then I carried off his goods and plundered his cattle."

dependent, minor operations. The pharaoh's vizier [equivalent to the Assyrian field marshal] acted as war minister. . . . The field army consisted of divisions of about 5,000 men . . . though the number may have varied depending on the occasion. . . . The commanding officer of a division had twenty company commanders (the "standard bearers"), and each company consisted of 250 men. Companies were divided into units of fifty men each under platoon leaders known as "the great ones of the fifty."[17]

Once the units of a Near Eastern army reached the battlefield, the high-ranking officers organized them into formations—mainly lines and columns—designed to facilitate either attack or defense. Evidence suggests that the Sumerians pioneered many formations and tactics that were used later throughout the region and beyond. At least by 2500 B.C., they used both light and heavy infantry (foot soldiers), for example. The terms *light* and *heavy* refer to the use of armor, light infantry having little or no armor and heavy infantry wearing body armor and helmets. Generally speaking, heavy infantry made direct contact the enemy, while light infantry fought more at a distance using missile weapons. Surviving sculptures show that Sumerian light infantry wore no protective armor and carried no shields. Each man held a javelin and a battle-ax. Apparently a line of these troops approached the enemy, at a given signal threw their javelins, and then closed with the enemy lines and fought hand to hand with their axes.

By contrast, the heavy infantry, in metal helmets and heavy leather cloaks (sometimes studded with metal disks), wielded

This section of the Vulture Stele shows a closely packed formation of heavy infantrymen.

long spears and large shields stretching from shoulder to ankle. One carving, the Vulture Stele (so-called because it shows enemy dead being picked at by vultures), shows a tightly packed formation of such heavy infantry marching toward an enemy. The men in the front rank hold up their shields, creating a protective barrier. The soldiers behind them project their spears forward through the spaces between the shields, making the unit even more formidable. Such a formation was designed either to mow down or to scare off enemy forces. To effectively maneuver and fight in such specialized formations takes a great deal of drill and practice, so at least some of the soldiers of that time must have formed a hard core of full-time professionals. (The rest were drafted into temporary service when needed.)

DEVELOPMENT OF WAR CHARIOTS

Heavy infantry and professional troops were not the only military innovations introduced by the Sumerians. By the mid–third millennium B.C. at the latest, they had also invented the war chariot, which went on to revolutionize warfare in the Near East. Generals increasingly designed the formations and tactics of ordinary foot soldiers around those of central strike forces made up of chariots. (It is important to note that chariots were very expensive to build and maintain; therefore, only large, wealthy states, like Babylonia, Assyria, and Egypt, could afford chariot corps with thousands of vehicles.)

These early chariots were crude by later standards. It would be more accurate to call them "battle-wagons," as they consisted of solid-wheeled carts pulled by four donkeys. (Horses were not yet widely used in the Near East.) Such vehicles were heavy, clumsy, and hard to maneuver, and donkeys are not strong or fast runners. At first, therefore, the use of chariots in battle must have been rather limited. Most scholars think they were mainly "prestige" vehicles for carrying the king and his officers to and from the battlefield.

Still, the seeds had been planted for the development of a devastating new mode of warfare. That development was made possible by two major new innovations in the early second millennium B.C. One was the widespread domestication of the horse, which was much stronger and faster than the donkey. The other was the perfection of woodworking methods that produced wheels with spokes and lightweight chariot bodies. The combination of faster draft animals and lighter vehicles opened the way for charges of massed chariots on infantry. Thus, by the mid–second millennium B.C. all the great powers of the Near East had large chariot corps.

THE COMPOSITE BOW

Another major military innovation of the early second millennium B.C., the composite bow, supplemented chariot warfare and made it more devastating. As Trevor Watkins

A LIGHTWEIGHT EGYPTIAN CHARIOT

In this excerpt from volume 1 of The Art of Warfare in Biblical Lands in the Light of Archaeological Study, *modern Near Eastern scholar Yigael Yadin describes a surviving Egyptian chariot dating to about 1500 B.C.*

"This chariot has three main elements: the body, the wheels, and the pole and yoke. The body has a wooden frame. . . . Its base is one meter [3.3 feet] wide and half a meter deep. It is 75 centimeters [29 inches] high in the front—which would cover about half way up to the thighs of the charioteer. . . . The whole of the front and the bottom part of the sides of the body were [covered by leather]. The axel-rod is 6 centimeters [2.4 inches] thick at the center and its length between the wheels is 1.23 meters [4.1 feet]. . . . The wheels had four spokes. . . . Everything was planned to make the vehicle light, flexible, and strong."

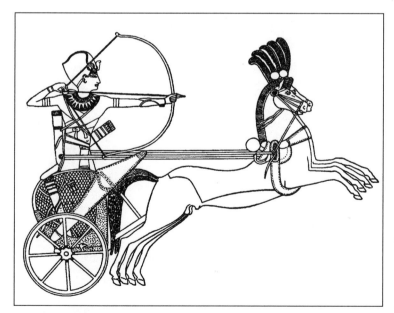

An Egyptian charioteer with his rig and weapons, as they appeared in the New Kingdom.

puts it, the new weapon "introduced a rapid-fire missile delivery system necessary for mounting on the fast new chariots."[18] Primitive versions of the composite bow, which combines several different materials to produce a more powerful spring, had been known for centuries, especially in parts of central Asia. "Among the Serovo hunters of the Lena Valley, Siberia," for instance, military historian William Reid points out, "a composite bow was in use in the third millennium B.C. that reveals a . . . technique for stiffening the bow with splinters of antler, and creating additional resilience [spring] by backing it with sinew."[19]

Some breakthrough that has not yet been identified by scholars occurred in Meso-potamia that made composite bows significantly more powerful and practical. What *is* known is that the four primary materials of this newer version were wood, animal horn, sinew, and glue. Even the wooden portions were often made up of two to four kinds of wood, each having certain desired elastic properties. The weapon could fire an arrow up to 600 yards or more; however, even the best archers could not achieve effective accuracy beyond 150 or 200 yards. Nevertheless, the new bow could fire arrows faster and at higher velocities than the traditional simple bow. Skilled archers standing in chariots could get closer to enemy lines and do more damage, even when the opposing troops had shields.

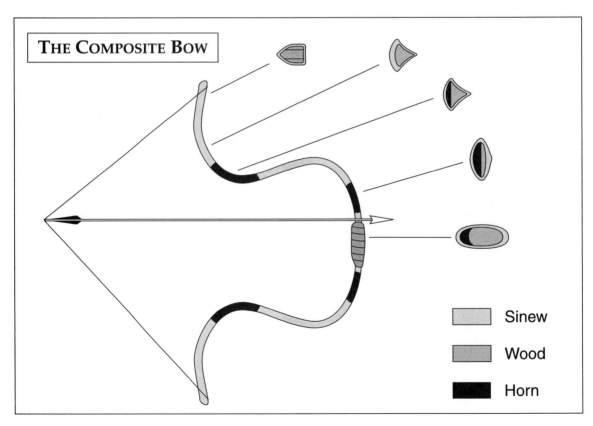

THE COMPOSITE BOW

Sinew

Wood

Horn

At the same time, military strategists did not overlook the new bows' potential for foot soldiers as well. They developed a battlefield formation built around a tactical field unit known as the archer pair. In this arrangement, brought to perfection by the Assyrians, one of the two men held a large shield to protect against incoming arrows and other missiles. The second man, the archer, hid with his companion behind the shield and fired off one arrow after another. Rows of hundreds or thousands of these pairs moved forward in unison during a battle, wreaking havoc on enemy lines.

ARMIES ON THE ATTACK

Though they were frequently the centerpiece of an army on the attack, the chariots and archer pairs were also part of a larger, integrated army. That is, they acted in concert with large numbers of light infantry armed in various ways. The weapons wielded by the light infantry were a combination of old and new. The mace had, by this time, been phased out because it could not penetrate the metal helmets now worn by a majority of soldiers. Battle-axes remained standard, however, as did spears, javelins, and daggers. Meanwhile, the increasing production of better-quality bronze made sword blades stronger, so swords became more common on the battlefield. One particularly useful sword, which the Egyptians called the *khopesh*, was in wide use across the Near East by 1600 B.C. Its curved blade resembled those of sickles used to cut wheat, and, like a sickle, it was very effective for slashing.

The way that foot soldiers bearing these weapons worked in conjunction with chariots is not completely clear, and, in any case, likely varied from one place and time to another. Probably the most common approach was for foot archers to soften up the enemy. Then the archers would retire to make way for the chariot charge. Right behind the chariots came groups of light infantry called "runners," whose jobs were to clear the field of capsized chariots, capture or kill fallen enemy archers, and rescue their own fallen bowmen. The runners also attacked any enemy infantry who were supporting the opposing chariots.

The loser of such a battle often retreated to a nearby city, where tall, sturdy defensive walls afforded considerable protection. To counter such moves and gain access to enemy cities, Near Eastern armies perfected an offensive mode of warfare that had been developing since Neolithic times—siege tactics. The Assyrians became especially adept at prosecuting sieges. Noted historian D.J. Wiseman describes their typical methods:

> A ramp or causeway of piled up earth, rubble or wood enabled the attacker to gain closer access to the upper, more penetrable and fragile walls. A battering ram was brought up . . . a ram of metal-tipped wood housed in a wooden framework shielded by a covering. It was propelled on wheels or foot to dislodge the upper brickwork [of the walls] or smash down gateways or weak places. Attempts by defenders to set fire to these machines and the ramp by pouring burning oil or torches down on them usually failed, for the Assyrians devised

This detail from a wall carving in the mortuary temple of Rameses II shows two Egyptian charioteers in the midst of the battle of Kadesh.

contraptions to dowse the canopy with water. . . . Where the objective lay by a river, the Assyrians used a siege tower [a large wooden framework that could be moved on wheels or rollers and carried soldiers and weapons]. Constructed upstream and floated into position, this gave a field of fire down onto the defenders within the walls. . . . Meanwhile sappers [miners], covered by bowmen and shields, attempted to tunnel and undermine the walls.[20]

THE FIRST RECORDED BATTLE

Most of these military units and tactics—light infantry, archers, chariot corps, and sieges—came into play in the earliest large military campaign and battle in world history for which surviving records give spe-

cific details. The Battle of Kadesh took place in Syria in about 1274 B.C. The Egyptians, led by the pharaoh Rameses II, squared off against the Hittites (from Asia Minor), commanded by their king, Muwatallis. Modern estimates for the sizes of the opposing forces are 2,500 chariots and 37,000 infantry on the Hittites' side and 2,000 chariots and 18,000 foot soldiers in the Egyptian ranks.

The outcome of the battle was indecisive. But, clearly, the size, complexity, and firepower of elite armies had become far more formidable than any seen in Neolithic times. Indeed, the forces commanded by Rameses and Muwatallis were state-of-the-art for their time. Yet the evolution of warfare had in many ways just begun. Soon, hundreds of miles to the west, the Greeks and Romans would build military machines that would humble and crush those of Egypt and its neighbors.

3 Greece and Rome at War: The Rise of the West

History is filled with surprises and unexpected turns of events. The earliest major innovations in large-scale warfare, including metal weapons, heavy infantry, chariots, and the rise of empires, occurred in Asia, particularly the Near East. Yet Eastern military traditions were eventually eclipsed by those of Western, or European-based, civilization. Through exploration, colonization, conquest, and other means, Western nations like Spain, France, Britain, and the United States achieved political or economic dominance over most of the world in modern times.

The West's phenomenal success was due in large part to the effectiveness of its weapons and military traditions and tactics. And these, Victor Hanson points out, can be traced back to "a series of practices created at the beginning of Western culture by the Greeks." It was, he says, a military legacy

> fundamental to the expansion and survival of the later West. . . . The Greeks created a unique approach to organized fighting that . . . proved to be the most lethal brand of warfare in the Mediterranean, the chief tenets of which have characterized Western military tradition ever since. [21]

Indeed, the Greeks introduced the most efficient and devastating heavy infantry the world had yet seen, as well as important new tactics and technological advances. Another Western people, the Romans, copied and then improved on and surpassed these innovations. Rome created the greatest military machine of ancient times. And with its highly trained, disciplined, and seasoned troops, it conquered and absorbed the Greek city-states and kingdoms, along with the rest of southern Europe. In its turn, when it fell in the fifth and sixth centuries, Rome passed along the formidable Greco-Roman military tradition to later Western peoples and nations.

THE HOPLITE AND HIS ARMS

The beginnings of that tradition date from about the eighth century B.C., when Greece was emerging from a long period of poverty and illiteracy and independent city-states were forming across the Greek sphere. Greece was never a unified country in ancient times. Instead, it comprised hundreds of small city-states, each of which viewed itself as a separate nation. Each city-state resolutely defended its territory

REASONS FOR WESTERN MILITARY SUCCESS

In The Wars of the Ancient Greeks, *noted historian Victor D. Hanson lists these eight general military customs and beliefs pioneered by the Greeks, which contributed to the later military triumph of the West.*

"1. Advanced technology: The unsurpassed excellence of both weapons and armor.

2. Superior discipline: Effective training and ready acceptance of command.

3. Ingenuity in response: An intellectual tradition . . . that sought constant improvement in the face of challenge.

4. The creation of a broad, shared military observance among the majority of the population: The preference for citizen militias and civilian participation in military decision-making.

5. Choice of decisive engagement: The preference to meet the enemy head-on . . . and to resolve the fighting as quickly and decisively as possible.

6. Dominance of infantry: The notion that property-owners on foot with muscular strength . . . alone win wars.

7. A systematic application of capital to warmaking: The ability to . . . [raise enough money to field armies] for extensive periods of time.

8. A moral opposition to militarism: [The demand by the people that wars be justified.]"

and way of life with a small army made up mostly of farmers who doubled as soldiers only when needed. Also, most of the Greek states had citizen assemblies where the fighting men could choose or at least shape the policies of their leaders. This created a new breed of soldier—an independent-thinking, self-reliant, patriotic individual who was ready to defend his property and his state with tenacity and zeal.

By the beginning of the seventh century B.C., a unique mode of warfare based on these small citizen militias had become widespread in the Greek sphere. The new system was built around heavily armored infantry soldiers called hoplites. (The term *hoplite* may derive from the Greek word *hopla,* meaning "heavy equipment.") A hoplite's extensive array of arms and armor was collectively called the panoply. One of the most important elements of the panoply was the shield, the *hoplon* (or *aspis*), which was about three feet in diameter and weighed seventeen pounds. It was composed of a wooden core reinforced on the outside by a coating of bronze (or layers of ox hide). The inside of the shield had a distinctive gripping system. The hoplite passed his left forearm through a bronze strip with a loop in the middle and grasped a leather handle with his left hand. This allowed him to let go of the handle and hold a spare weapon in his left hand without losing his shield; it also helped to relieve the burden of the shield's considerable weight.

To protect his chest and abdomen, a hoplite wore a cuirass. If he could afford it, it might be of high-quality bronze, which was very expensive. The most common type was made up of several layers of linen or canvas glued together to form a stiff shirt. Sometimes the outer layer was covered with metal plates or scales.

The other elements of the panoply included a bronze helmet, which had eye slits and breathing spaces for the nose and mouth. Some helmets featured movable visors or cheek pieces; others had decorative plumes of horse hair attached to the top. A hoplite also wore greaves, bronze lower-leg protectors. As for weapons, he wielded a thrusting spear about seven feet long with an iron head and a sword with an iron blade about two feet long. Though it could be lethal, the sword was mainly a backup weapon used when a fighter lost or broke his spear.

THE IRRESISTIBLE PHALANX

Even more formidable than the hoplite's panoply was the formation in which he fought. Known as the phalanx, in some

This and other scenes from the 1962 film The Three Hundred Spartans *accurately reproduce the Greek phalanx's formidable barrier of shields and spears.*

ways it resembled the formation used by the Sumerian infantry in the Vulture Stele. However, the Greek version was much better armored and benefited from more depth and cohesion. It consisted of a long block of soldiers standing in ranks (lines), one behind the other. Eight ranks was the average depth, but sometimes generals called for more or fewer, as in the case of the Athenian commander at the Battle of Marathon, in 490 B.C. Facing a considerably larger army of invading Persians (whose empire was centered in the Near East), he thinned the center of his battle line to four or fewer ranks; this allowed him to match the enemy's mile-wide front line and

Members of a phalanx march toward the enemy in open order. Before attacking, they will close ranks.

ensured that the Persians could not outflank his phalanx.

The tremendous offensive capabilities of the Greek phalanx derived from two inherent qualities. First, it provided each hoplite with a great deal of protection. When assembled in close order, about two to three feet apart, the fighters' uplifted shields formed an unbroken protective barrier. Second, as the hoplites marched forward in unison, the formation took on an enormous amount of momentum, which increased still further when it made contact with the en-

THE PHALANX

Open Phalanx
5–6 feet between soldiers

Closed Phalanx
When maneuvering into battle the rear half of each file moves forward to create a "shield wall."

emy line. At this point, the hoplites in the front rank jabbed their spears at their opponents. Meanwhile, the Greeks in the rear ranks pushed at their comrades' backs, shoving them forward with irresistible force.

The phalanx was especially effective when used against non-Greeks. (When two Greek phalanxes met head-on, the result was usually an immense shoving match that ended when one side became exhausted and retreated.) The contest at Marathon was typical. At first, the Persians pushed back the thin Athenian center. But then the Athenian wings, each forming a small phalanx, turned inward on the Persian center and, like living steamrollers, crushed all in their path.

The phalanx became even more formidable in the fourth century B.C. Philip II, king of the northern Greek state of Macedonia, further increased the formation's depth and replaced the spears of the men in the rear ranks with battle pikes (long spears). These protruded from the front of the formation, often called the "Macedonian phalanx," creating an impenetrable and frightening mass of iron spear points. It is no wonder, then, that the second-century B.C. Greek historian Polybius said, "So long as the phalanx retains its characteristic form and strength, nothing can withstand its charge or resist it face to face."[22]

CAVALRY AND LIGHT INFANTRY

In one form or another, the phalanx remained the central feature of Greek armies. However, other kinds of soldiers supported the hoplites in secondary roles. At first, the Greeks made

A companion cavalryman in the army of Macedonian rulers Philip and Alexander. These horsemen charged directly at infantry.

little or no use of cavalry (mounted warriors), which came into common use only in the late fifth century B.C. during the Peloponnesian War. (This was a long, bloody conflict in which most of the Greek states fought one another.) Even then, horsemen were not employed in direct charges on the infantry. Saddles were crude and stirrups did not yet exist, so staying on a swiftly moving horse was difficult, especially if the rider was loaded down with armor and weapons. For centuries, therefore, cavalrymen, wearing little or no armor, primarily protected the wings of the phalanx from enemy flanking movements or chased down escaping enemy troops after the battle was over.

Greek cavalry finally came into its own under Philip II and his son, Alexander III (who later came to be called "the Great"). Shortly before conquering most of Greece in the mid–fourth century B.C., Philip created a highly effective integrated arms system in which the phalanx, cavalry, and light infantry all played key roles in battle. His elite cavalry corps consisted of young Macedonian noblemen, who wore bronze armor. Called the "companion cavalry," this unit often charged in a wedge-shaped formation directly into enemy infantry. These horsemen could not defeat a phalanx or other large formation alone. However, they could create a breach in the enemy line large enough for the Macedonian phalanx to enter and slice the enemy army in half.

Light infantry, or skirmishers, also played a role, both before and after Philip and Alexander. Such fighters, who wore little or no armor, included archers, slingers, and peltasts. The latter carried small bundles of javelins, which they threw at the enemy and then ran away. Softening up the enemy this way before the charge of the phalanx was one of the two jobs of skirmishers, the other being to protect the sides and rear of the phalanx. As happened with cavalry, the Greek states made little use of skirmishers until the Peloponnesian War. From that time on, most were mercenaries (hired soldiers) from fringe areas of the Greek sphere.

Naval Warfare

The Greek military system quickly proved to be the finest in the world. After their hu-

miliating loss at Marathon, the Persians retreated, but ten years later they returned to Greece with an army of 200,000, the largest ever fielded in ancient times. Though vastly outnumbered, the Greeks decisively defeated the invaders in a series of battles. Later, in 334 B.C., shortly after Philip's death, Alexander led a united Greek army into the Near East and brought the Persian Empire, the mightiest in the world, to its knees in only a decade.

During these centuries, the Greeks, who had long been ardent, skilled sailors, supplemented their land forces by making effective use of ships, as both troop transports and offensive weapons. Indeed, the key event in halting the Persian invasion in 480 B.C. was the Battle of Salamis, fought in a bay southwest of Athens. The victory was so overwhelming that it gave the Greeks effective naval superiority over the eastern Mediterranean region for three centuries to come.

The Greek vessels that fought at Salamis and in later sea battles were mostly triremes, the most common warship of the age. A typical trireme was about 130 feet long, 18 feet wide, and featured three banks of oars—62 in the upper bank, and 54 each in the middle and lower banks. Such a ship carried a total crew of about 200. This included 170 rowers (who were not slaves, as often depicted in movies, but free Greek citizens) and 15 deckhands. Also on board were 15 hoplite marines and archers, who did the actual fighting. (Sometimes up to 40 marines were used.)

Greek warships could not remain at sea for long periods, mainly because they lacked eating and sleeping facilities. So they had to dock or be dragged ashore at least once a day.

As a result, naval strategy was, of necessity, short-term in nature and built around winning an individual battle. The tactics were fairly straightforward, the most common consisting of ramming an enemy vessel with a bronze-coated "beak" mounted on the front of the trireme. Another effective maneuver was for two ships to attack the enemy at once.

The first approached at an angle and sheared off the opponent's oars, after which the second came straight on and rammed the exposed hull. The Greeks also used grappling hooks or ropes to bring an enemy vessel alongside their own. The hoplite marines then boarded the opposing ship and engaged its crew hand to hand.

THE GREEK VICTORY AT SALAMIS

In his play The Persians *(472 B.C.), the Athenian playwright Aeschylus recounts the sea battle at Salamis, in which he fought. In this excerpt (from Philip Vellacott's translation), a messenger describes the scene to the Persian queen mother.*

"Then from the Greek ships rose like a song of joy the piercing battle-cry. . . . The Persians knew their error; fear gripped every man. They were no fugitives who sang that terrifying paean [battle hymn], but Greeks charging with courageous hearts to battle. . . . A Greek ship charged first, and chopped off the whole stern of a Persian galley. Then charge followed charge on every side. . . . In that narrow space, our ships were jammed in hundreds; none could help another. They rammed each other . . . and some were stripped of every oar.

Meanwhile the enemy came round us in a ring and charged. Our vessels heeled over; the sea was hidden, carpeted with wrecks and dead men; all the shores and reefs were full of dead. . . . The Greeks seized fragments of wrecks and broken oars and hacked and stabbed at our men swimming in the sea. . . . The whole sea was one din of shrieks and dying groans, till night and darkness hid the scene."

Triremes like this one won the battle at Salamis.

The Roman Manipular System

While Greek armies and navies were gaining mastery of the eastern Mediterranean and parts of the Near East, hundreds of miles to the west a hardy, incredibly resilient people were rising to prominence. The Romans, at first, controlled only a tiny patch of west-central Italy. By 265 B.C., however, they had conquered nearly all of the peninsula. The following year they declared war on Carthage, a powerful maritime em-

Roman legionaries of the Punic Wars era brandish their weapons.

pire centered in North Africa; and there followed three conflicts with Carthage (the Punic Wars), all of which Rome won. Having gained dominance over the western Mediterranean, in 200 B.C. the Romans turned on the Greek lands of the sea's eastern sector.

What was the nature of this army that had achieved such spectacular success and now challenged the proven Greek military system? When Rome was still a moderate-sized city-state, it had utilized the hoplite phalanx, which it and other Italian states had copied from the Greeks. (The Romans collectively called the phalanx and the light-armed troops that supported it a legion; Roman soldiers were called legionaries.) In 390 B.C., however, the Romans suffered a disastrous defeat at the hands of an invading force of Gauls, a tribal people from the region north of the Alps. Believing that the phalanx had been too rigid and inflexible, over the next two generations Rome abandoned and replaced it.

In the new system, a legion broke down into several smaller battlefield units called maniples (meaning "handfuls" in Latin). Each maniple could act independently of the others and also combine with them in various ways. This imparted more flexibility to the army during battle. The military reformers also replaced the round hoplite shield with a larger oval-shaped (later rectangular) one called the *scutum*, which provided even better protection. Each Roman legionary also received two short javelins, one heavy and one light, and a superb thrusting sword.

These weapons were integral to the special tactics of the manipular system (named

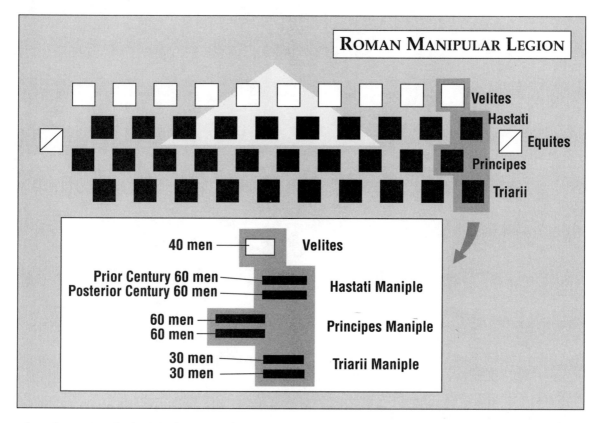

ROMAN MANIPULAR LEGION

- Velites
- Hastati
- Equites
- Principes
- Triarii

40 men — Velites

Prior Century 60 men
Posterior Century 60 men — Hastati Maniple

60 men
60 men — Principes Maniple

30 men
30 men — Triarii Maniple

after the maniples). On the battlefield, the infantry stood in three long lines of maniples, one behind the other, with spaces separating one maniple from another. As the battle commenced, the men in the front maniples spread out, forming a solid bank of soldiers, and charged. At a distance of roughly a hundred feet from the enemy line, the legionaries hurled their light javelins and quickly followed with their heavy ones. Still running, they then drew their swords and smashed into the opposing ranks. If these troops failed to defeat the enemy, they retreated, and the second line of maniples spread out and charged. Meanwhile, the men who had already fought rested in case they were needed for a third charge. If the Roman commander decided victory was

not possible, the fresh legionaries in the third line of maniples formed a solid bank, raised their shields, and pointed their spears forward in phalanx fashion. Behind this barrier, the rest of the army retreated in an orderly manner.

EXPANSION, DECLINE, AND OBLIVION

The first pivotal showdown between Rome's new military system and the older Greek system occurred in 197 B.C. at Cynoscephalae, a steep hill in central Greece. In a furious, chaotic battle, the Roman maniples proved far more flexible than the cumbersome Macedonian phalanx.

The Romans became extremely adept at carrying out sieges. Here, Roman soldiers use catapults and other devices to capture a city.

Suddenly beset by enemy maniples in their rear, the Greek fighters were unable to swing their tall pikes around fast enough and were slaughtered in huge numbers. Other disastrous Greek defeats followed, all confirming the superiority of the Roman military. By 146 B.C., Rome was master of most of the Greek lands.

In the centuries that followed, the Romans instituted more military reforms, making their army even more efficient and formidable. They replaced their maniples with larger, stronger battlefield units called cohorts, but kept the same flexibility. They also made their soldiers full-time professionals who trained and drilled for long periods and gained years of practical experience.

In addition, after borrowing basic siege techniques from the Greeks, the Romans raised the art of siege warfare to new heights. "The legions had the ability to surround completely a besieged city with camps, pickets, and ditches," says military historian Simon Anglim.

> While other armies were content with a blockade that cut off the main gates and roads, and then patrolled the perimeter, the Romans made sure to bar all methods of escape with an unbroken line of [siege] works.[23]

Rome's army was so tough, disciplined, and effective that it allowed the Roman Empire to expand and then maintain itself for several centuries. When that army declined in size, discipline, and efficiency in the fourth and fifth centuries A.D., however, the Empire was doomed. Invaders from central and northern Europe steadily forged kingdoms in former Roman territories, some of which became the seedlings for the later nations of Europe. The old Greco-Roman world faded into oblivion. But many of its cultural traditions, including military ones, lived on to shape the future course of the West.

Chapter

4 Knights and Castles in Medieval Europe and Japan

After the fall of Rome, Europe entered the medieval period (also called the Middle Ages), lasting from about 600 to 1650. The state of military arts and technology around the world during this era shows that warfare was developing at markedly different rates in different regions. At first, Europe was not significantly ahead of all the others. The infant medieval European kingdoms had inherited many advanced military ideas from the Greeks and Romans. Yet the transmission of this legacy was informal and haphazard. And, for a long time, Europeans applied these ideas in a less organized manner and on a decidedly smaller scale than the Greeks and Romans had. Only toward the end of medieval times, when armies became larger and better organized and guns began to be used in battle, did the West begin to fulfill its great military potential. "Quite without fully understanding the extent of their achievements," military historian Christon I. Archer points out, "Europeans developed weapons and technology that before long allowed them to dominate, or at least to influence, all other civilizations around the globe." [24]

Meanwhile, from a military standpoint, most other parts of the world were either far behind Europe as the medieval period

began or steadily fell behind it over time. When Europeans were warring with crossbows, catapults, and primitive firearms, for example, the Native Americans were still fighting with Stone Age weapons. On the other hand, China possessed military traditions and potential equal to those of medieval Europe for several centuries. The Chinese even experimented with gunpowder and firearms before the Europeans did. Yet China fell behind because its cultural traditions discouraged military innovation and expansion. In China, Archer explains,

> peaceful order, scholarship, bureaucratic control, [and] self-discipline were all extolled above warfare and the military as ideals. . . . In this atmosphere, military technology was seen as a low priority . . . and the status quo [was] more important than technical development. [25]

By contrast, military innovations in another Eastern society, Japan, were encouraged. Moreover, during the medieval period Japan developed a feudal society similar in many ways to that of Europe. Eventually, the Japanese, like the Chinese, fell back on tradition and allowed military progress to stagnate. But a brief examination of the situation in medieval Europe and Japan reveals how, at least for a while, several aspects of warfare, including castles and mounted knights, developed in parallel in the West and the East.

MEDIEVAL EUROPEAN CAVALRY

Cavalry composed of mounted knights was a case in point. Armored knights did not dominate European warfare in the period as scholars once thought. But they did play a key role, not only on the battlefield but also in the system of feudalism, which supplied most of the soldiers who fought the wars.

Feudalism, which had taken firm hold in Europe by the eleventh century, was built on allegiance and service to local noble families. After the fall of Rome's large, centralized empire, European society became more localized in character, as numerous kings, princes, dukes, and other nobles had power only over their own small kingdoms or large estates. A free man provided his noble lord with military service and in exchange received a piece of land. Soldiers who worked for and were dependent on a noble were known as retainers (or vassals).

Many of the more well-to-do retainers became knights. Indeed, they and the nobles were the only ones who *could* become knights, because raising horses and equipping and training mounted warriors were very expensive endeavors. Not surprisingly, such cavalrymen gained increasing social status and wealth and became an elite class of fighters.

The rise of the knightly class in warfare and society did not occur all at once, however. Early medieval cavalrymen were not nearly as impressive or formidable as later ones. At first, mounted fighters wore light armor made of mail, rows of iron rings or scales either riveted or sewn together to form a heavy protective shirt. (They inherited mail from the Romans, who had used it for many centuries.) Mail was fairly lightweight and flexible. But the protection it offered was minimal, since it could not stop the direct thrust of a sword, lance, or arrow.

For weapons, these early knights mainly wielded swords and spears (and sometimes bows). They rarely made charges on either cavalry or infantry. Instead, they

Heavily armored knights like this one first appeared in the late thirteenth century.

These drawings show various types of armor used by medieval European warriors. Most wear suits of mail and all carry protective metal shields.

acted as scouts, guarded the flanks of traveling armies, raided villages, and pursued fleeing enemies. Also, at crucial moments in battle the cavalrymen dismounted and fought on foot.

Later, in the period of the eleventh to sixteenth centuries, mounted fighters became much more heavily armored. Their mail shirts became longer and heavier, for example, and mail protected their heads, arms, hands, and legs. As the rapid multiplication of armor continued, many knights started wearing iron caps under their headmail or single-piece metal helmets over the mail. And between 1200 and 1250, metalplated body armor was introduced for both men and horses.

As for weapons, heavily armored knights discarded spears and bows and adopted long iron swords. They also used the lance, a pole about ten to twelve feet long that broadened into a flared hand guard in the back. The addition of two crucial inventions—the stirrup and the wraparound saddle—gave knights more stability atop their mounts and made cavalry charges with leveled lances a formidable offensive tactic.

MEDIEVAL FOOT SOLDIERS AND THEIR WEAPONS

The most effective use of such heavy cavalry was against infantry. Foot soldiers, including archers, swordsmen, spearmen, pikemen, and others, played an important role in warfare throughout the medieval period. Under the feudal system, each country estate owned by a retainer or other supporter of the leading noble had to supply a group of soldiers, drafted mainly from the peasantry, for the noble's army during wartime. The nobles also supplemented their local infantry with mercenaries, who were better armed and trained and more battle hardened than peasants.

In general the foot soldiers wore much less armor than cavalrymen did. Most infantrymen could not afford elaborate armor. And in any case, such heavy protection would have weighed them down too much in battle. The most common infantry armor consisted of a light mail shirt and a metal helmet, often in the form of an iron cap with a wide brim.

Medieval foot soldiers used a variety of weapons that varied from place to place and era to era. Among these were swords, daggers, spears, pikes, axes, maces, simple bows, crossbows, and eventually crude handguns. One of the more effective weapons of the period was the English longbow. Although it did not shoot arrows as far as a crossbow, a longbowman could fire several arrows in the same amount of time that a crossbowman fired one. The longbow proved itself again and again, especially during the Hundred Years' War, fought between England and France from 1337 to 1453. At Crécy, in 1346, for example, massed English longbows won the day over the French knights and their support troops.

In the last few medieval centuries, two other infantry weapons, the pike and handheld firearm, became increasingly effective. Inspired by the ancient Greeks, in the twelfth and thirteenth centuries the Scots and Swiss began developing phalanx-like units in which the soldiers wielded long battle pikes. The Swiss pikes eventually measured eighteen feet in length. When the Swiss phalanx, called the Gewalthaufen, went on the offensive, it was extremely difficult to stop, and the Swiss infantry remained Europe's finest until nearly the end of medieval times.

Early firearms worked in conjunction with pikes in late medieval battles. The first European weapons utilizing gunpowder, which appeared in the 1300s, were very crude. The earliest cannons, for instance, were so heavy and immobile and took so long to load that they were of little use on the battlefield. Early handheld guns had similar limitations. It required many technological advances over the course of nearly four centuries for firearms to reach the point where they dominated warfare. So it was not unusual for generals as late as the 1500s and early 1600s to combine units of men wielding primitive muskets (handheld firearms) with units of pikemen. The musketeers with their slow-loading weapons stood inside a protective barrier of pikemen, who kept the enemy at bay while the gunmen reloaded.

CASTLES AND SIEGES

Whatever weapons and tactics were used, battles involving cavalry or infantry or both were not nearly as common in medieval Europe as sieges of castles. Indeed, castles dominated military affairs, partly because they were the residences of leading nobles and centers of their political, economic, and

EARLY HANDHELD GUNS

The first handheld firearms consisted of bronze or brass tubes between eight and twelve feet long. These were so heavy and awkward that they had to be rested on a pole to fire. Typically, the operator poured gunpowder into the front of the barrel, rammed the powder down tight with a stick, and then added a small piece of wood and a lead ball. To ignite the powder, the gunner inserted a red-hot wire through a small hole bored into the barrel.

Steady advancements followed. In the early 1400s, the weapon became shorter and lighter so that the gunner could hold it on his shoulder or under his arm when firing. Then came the introduction of the matchlock mechanism in the mid to late 1400s. A metal lever bolted to the top of the barrel held the match, a smoldering piece of rope, in place. When the gunner pulled the trigger, a spring snapped the lever back so that the match touched and ignited a small amount of powder in a tiny pan. The flash then penetrated a hole in the barrel, igniting the powder inside and firing the gun. By about 1500, a portable matchlock, widely called a harquebus, was a common infantry weapon in many parts of Europe.

Modern reenactors prepare their matchlock guns for a mock battle. The first handheld guns were heavy and time-consuming to load.

military power. As scholar Christopher Gravett puts it:

> Castles controlled the countryside around them; they provided bases from which . . . squadrons of knights could ride out to attack an enemy. . . . Further, castles were often situated on roads or rivers and frequently near junctions; therefore . . . in order to secure a conquered country, the castles themselves had to be captured.[26]

Medieval siege warfare had two main aspects—defense and offense, that is, protection for the besieged and capture by the besiegers. The first primitive castles, constructed mainly of wood, were erected in northern France in the late ninth and early tenth centuries. Soon afterward, feudal lords grew more numerous and more powerful. And from the eleventh century on, larger and stronger stone castles rapidly spread across Europe.

The defensive features of these structures were influenced by those of existing stone fortifications at Constantinople and other strategic locations in the Near East (which were based on ancient Greco-Roman models). One such feature was machicolation, the outward projection of a wall at the top of the battlements. Through openings in the floors of such projections, the defenders dropped stones or boiling oil onto attackers. Most European castles also adopted the portcullis, a heavy vertical gateway door that moved up and down on chains attached to a winch located above the gate. Arrow loops were another common defensive feature of castles. They were narrow vertical wall slits through which defenders shot arrows at besiegers.

Such besiegers used a wide variety of weapons and techniques in their attempt to capture a castle. As in ancient times, foot soldiers often carried scaling ladders to the walls and attempted to climb them, an operation that always resulted in heavy casualties for the attackers. They

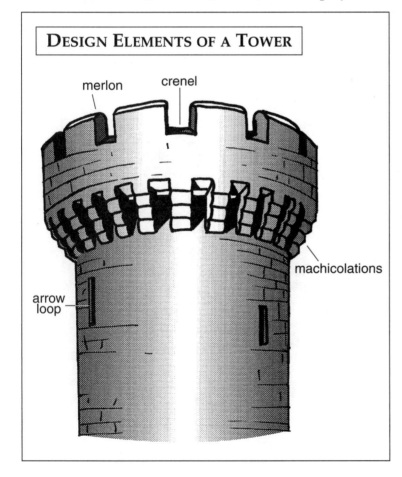

DESIGN ELEMENTS OF A TOWER

merlon

crenel

machicolations

arrow loop

A COUNTERWEIGHT DRAWBRIDGE

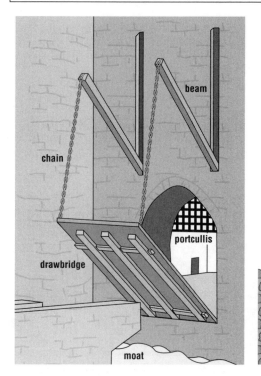

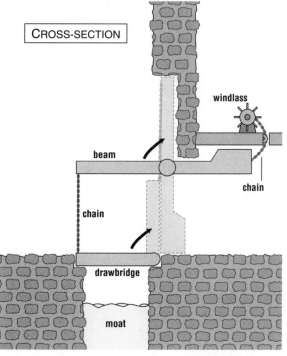

CROSS-SECTION

Some castle drawbridges operated by means of counterweights. The wooden drawbridge normally rested over the moat. To raise the bridge, defenders allowed the heavy rear ends of large beams to fall. As the lighter front ends rose, they raised the bridge by means of chains connecting the two.

also employed battering rams to smash down wooden gates. Meanwhile, crews of besiegers dug saps, or tunnels, under the castle's walls; these either caused a wall to collapse or provided access to the inside. Attackers tried to get over the walls as well by bringing up tall wooden siege towers, a few of which were truly enormous. One used in 1266 at the siege of Kenilworth Castle, in west-central England, held two hundred troops and eleven catapults.

Catapults were a kind of early artillery, a particularly effective class of offensive siege weapons. Other examples included the bal-

lista, a giant crossbow or spear thrower, and the trebuchet, a massive catapult-like device with a long leather sling attached to one end. A large trebuchet could toss a stone weighing half a ton as far as a quarter of a mile. Such artillery was also used to throw diseased animals into castles in hopes of infecting the defenders.

Eventually, another form of artillery—the cannon—was refined and perfected enough to make it the most formidable siege weapon yet contrived. Using the latest cannon technology, in 1494 France's King Charles VIII built forty-four cannons and invaded Italy.

A fortified medieval town comes under siege. A battering ram hammers the wall at left center, while a trebuchet is visible at lower right.

He swiftly reduced several castles to rubble, after which a number of nearby Italian city-states surrendered without a fight.

A CULTURE IN ISOLATION

The development of cannons and other firearms in Europe depended on knowledge of gunpowder, which had originally come from China. Similarly, many ideas for castle construction and siege devices had been inherited from Greece and Rome (by way of the medieval Near East). By contrast, faraway Japan, a group of islands off Asia's eastern coast, had developed in almost complete isolation; thus, its political, social, and military systems evolved with few or no outside influences. Yet incredibly, the Japanese developed feudalism and modes of warfare eerily similar to those of Europe in the very same period.

Indeed, by the eleventh century, when feudal lords were multiplying in Europe, powerful Japanese lords had collected groups of peasant vassals to work their lands. In exchange, the peasants received a lord's protection and a share of the food they grew. The military component of this arrangement took the form of warrior retainers known as samurai (meaning "those who serve").

The early samurai were well-to-do horsemen with high social status. They "formed a petty local aristocracy somewhat like the knights of early feudal Europe," noted scholar Edwin Reischauer explains, "for they too were mounted, armored warriors. Their chief weapons were the bow . . . skillfully used from horseback, and the curved steel sword, which came to be the finest blade in the world."[27] To the samurai, their swords were not mere weapons but also symbols of manhood and good character. This concept fit into a larger code of ethics that governed the thinking and conduct of the samurai. Like the code of chivalry sworn by some European knights, it emphasized honesty, reverence for parents and family, and loyalty to one's superiors, no matter how dire the danger.

JAPANESE FOOT SOLDIERS, CASTLES, AND GUNS

The heightened strictness and formality of samurai conduct in everyday life tended to spill over onto the battlefield. For example, it was common custom for a samurai warrior to introduce himself formally to the enemy, often as a challenge to one-on-one combat. Such a speech, given prior to a battle in 1184, has survived:

> Ho! I am Kajiwara Heizo Kagetoki, descended in the fifth generation from Gongoro Kagemasa of Kamakura, renowned warrior . . . and match for any thousand men! At the age of sixteen I rode [to a] siege . . . and, receiving an arrow in my left eye . . . I plucked it forth and with it shot down the marksman

who sent it, thereby gaining honors and leaving a name to posterity![28]

Although single combats among samurai were fairly common, they also fought in regular cavalry formations. These were very mobile and specialized in flanking movements and ambushes against infantry.

As in Europe, medieval Japanese infantry was composed mainly of farmers and other peasants fulfilling their duty to their lords, although over time some samurai became foot soldiers, too. By the 1400s, armies of infantry, armed with spears and bows, often numbered in the tens of thousands. This was as big as or bigger than most armies fielded in Europe in the same period.

Samurai foot soldiers prepare to attack in a scene from a modern film.

The major age of castle building in Japan came later, however. Between 1500 and 1600, numerous large castles were erected across Japan as powerful warlords battled for supremacy over the entire country. Like many European castles, which they closely resembled, the Japanese versions became economic centers and the nuclei of towns. According to a late-sixteenth-century document describing such a stronghold:

SCENE FROM A JAPANESE BATTLE

Medieval Japanese literature included stories of war and war heroes, including The Tale of the Heike, *written in the early 1200s. In this excerpt (quoted in Donald Keene's* Anthology of Japanese Literature *), a warrior named Kumagai encounters an enemy soldier at the end of a battle.*

"His eye fell on a single horseman who was attempting to reach one of the ships. . . . Kumagai beckoned him with his war fan, crying out: 'Shameful! to show an enemy your back. Return! Return!' The warrior turned his horse and rode back to the beach, where Kumagai at once engaged him in mortal combat. Quickly hurling him to the ground, he sprang upon him and tore off his helmet to cut off his head, when he beheld the face of a youth of sixteen . . . just about the age of his own son. . . . Kumagai was so overcome with compassion that he could scarcely wield his blade. . . . Weeping bitterly, he cut off the boy's head. 'Alas!' he cried, 'what life is so hard as that of a soldier?'"

Medieval Japanese cavalry charge the enemy in this scene from director Akira Kurosawa's magnificent 1985 film Ran.

Nijo Castle in Kyoto was built in 1603 to guard the city's imperial palace and to house Japan's military leader, the shogun, when he was in the area.

The main castle fronted on a river bank, the other sides being protected by moats and embankments. Around the castle were the dwellings of samurai, merchants, craftsmen . . . and peasants. The inner sector of the town was filled with inns, markets, and shops.[29]

During this same period, firearms appeared in Japan, thanks to Portuguese arms merchants. A few shrewd warlords quickly used these primitive muskets to bring their lesser rivals to their knees, and the whole country was united under one ruler by the 1590s. If Japan had remained open to out-side influences, it might have become a major world power like Spain, England, or France. Instead, however, the Japanese turned inward again. Fearing that foreigners would pollute the culture, they expelled them from the country in the early 1600s. In the years that followed, as Europe abandoned feudalism, Japan retained it. And the Japanese knew nothing about the industrial revolution and the new warfare technologies that were rapidly occurring on the outside. This proved a major factor in the increasing dominance of Western arms over Eastern ones.

5 The Fast, Fierce Armies of the Asian Conquerors

The course of military events in Japan and China was fairly typical of those in early Asian societies. Although Japanese and Chinese armies were often formidable, for the most part they fought on their own home grounds; their societies remained largely isolated from those of other lands and they showed little interest in foreign conquest. Indeed, only a few Eastern-based armies launched large-scale, continent-wide conquests in the medieval period. When they did, however, the results were extremely impressive. The most successful of all, the Mongols, for example, created the largest contiguous (territorially connected), land-based empire in history. Among the other successful Asian conquerors were the Huns, Arabs, and Magyars.

Although their motivations and objectives often differed, these and other similar Eastern groups had a number of military customs and methods in common. First, all used conventional, low-tech weapons such as bows, swords, and spears. This approach contrasted sharply with that of Western armies, which constantly strove to apply advancing technology to warfare. Also, with occasional exceptions, the armies of the Asian conquerors tended to be small, often as few as five to ten thousand men.

In addition, they lacked both training in and enthusiasm for siege warfare, a particular strength of the Western military tradition.

Yet the Asian conquerors amply made up for these disadvantages. Though small, their armies used horses superbly, so they were very mobile and fast, which allowed them to take full advantage of the element of surprise, as well as escape quickly from dangerous situations. Also, individual warriors were highly disciplined, physically tough, and able to survive on minimal rations. Sheer savagery was another key factor. Most of these armies (those of the Arabs being a notable exception) employed brutal tactics against civilians and soldiers alike, took few or no prisoners, and made highly effective use of terror tactics. None ever managed to seize Europe as a whole. But for a period of more than seven centuries, they controlled most of the vast known world bordering the relatively small European sphere.

THE SCOURGE OF GOD

The first warriors to sweep across Asia were the Huns, who originated somewhere in central Asia. In a way, they helped usher in the medieval period by setting in motion the greatest single series of folk migrations in history. About A.D. 370, they moved into what are now southern Russia and eastern Europe and drove the Goths and many other German tribes into the northern border provinces of the Roman Empire. This marked the beginning of the so-called barbarian invasions that eventually caused the fall of Rome and the rise of medieval European kingdoms.

Both the Germans and Romans viewed the Huns with fear and loathing. Some of the reasons for this appear in a graphic description penned by the fourth-century Roman historian Ammianus Marcellinus:

[The Huns] are quite abnormally savage. . . . They have squat bodies, strong limbs, and thick necks, and are so prodigiously ugly and bent that they might be two-legged animals, or the figures [gargoyles] crudely carved from stumps which are seen on the parapets of bridges. . . . Their way of life is so rough that they have no use for fire or seasoned food, but live on the roots of wild plants and the half-raw flesh of any sort of animals, which they warm a little by placing it between their thighs and the backs of their horses. . . . Once they have put their necks into some dingy shirt they never take it off or change it till it rots and falls to pieces. [30]

The Huns also inspired fear because of their distinctive mode of warfare and their excellent fighting skills. Their riding ability

A modern painting captures the ferocity of Attila and his Hunnish army ravaging the countryside. The Huns were among history's finest mounted warriors.

was so great that man and horse seemed to meld into a single, agile creature on the battlefield. Primarily horse archers, they used powerful composite bows, but also wielded lassos with the skill of rodeo cowboys. After throwing the enemy into confusion with these weapons, Hunnish warriors dismounted and attacked with heavy iron swords. "When they join battle," Ammianus wrote, summarizing their tactics,

> they advance in packs, uttering their various war cries. Being lightly equipped and very sudden in their movements, they can deliberately scatter and gallop about at random, inflicting tremendous slaughter. Their extreme nimbleness enables them to . . . pillage an enemy's camp before one catches sight of them.

. . . At close quarters, they fight without regard for their lives. [31]

Another common tactic used by the Huns, as well as later nomadic Asian warriors, was the false retreat; they appeared to flee, but later doubled back and surprised their opponents in an ambush.

The Huns also gained added cohesion and inspiration from an unusually talented and ruthless military leader and king—Attila. Rising to power in about 434, Attila took charge of the already large Hunnish empire that stretched from southern Russia to the Danube River in central Europe. The widespread killing, looting, and terror tactics employed by Attila's army earned him the nickname the "Scourge of God." Eventually, he grew bold enough to demand that the

This eighteenth-century engraving shows the Huns using their lassos in battle. They were also excellent archers who could shoot from the saddle.

THE MONGOL HORSE MESSENGERS

The leaders of the vast empire created by Genghis Khan relayed orders to and kept in touch with remote sections of the realm by employing a system of mounted horsemen called "arrow riders." Numbering as many as ten thousand at the height of the empire, they were selected from the strongest soldiers in the army. The arrow riders almost literally ate and slept in the saddle, which allowed them to cover more than a hundred miles per day. On main routes, the government set up posting stations about twenty-five miles apart, where the horsemen changed mounts, grabbed some food, and continued on their way at top speed. Each rider carried a bow, a small sword, and a dagger for protection in case he was attacked by bandits.

western Roman government give him half of the territory it then controlled. The Romans refused. And the following year, an army made up of Romans and Germans in a temporary alliance halted the Hunnish advance in a huge battle at Chalons (in northern France). Attila died about two years later. Without his guidance, his great realm, which had been loosely held together mostly by threats of violence, quickly disintegrated.

THE ARAB ARMIES

The tremendous speed with which the Huns swept across more than half a continent was duplicated on an even larger scale about two centuries later by the Arabs. Soon after the prophet Muhammad introduced a new faith—Islam—in Arabia in the early 600s and died in 632, his most zealous followers launched military campaigns into neighboring lands. In 634, the new caliph (meaning "successor" to Muhammad), Umar I, led an army into Palestine and then Syria. (At the time, Syria was controlled by the Byzantine Empire, centered at Constantinople.) By 637, the major Near Eastern cities of Jerusalem, Damascus, and Antioch had fallen to the Arabs. And by 651, Persia (now Iraq and Iran) had been defeated and absorbed. Arab armies also surged through Egypt, crossed North Africa, and entered Spain, where they established an Islamic state in 711.

These Arab armies achieved such phenomenal success in so little time for three reasons. The first was a matter of fortunate timing. As Christon Archer points out, the Arab expansion started "at a time when the Persian and Byzantine empires were in disarray," so most of the opponents the Arabs faced were disorganized and/or weak. "Equally important," Archer continues, was the fervor and devotion to duty of the Arabs themselves, who

> managed to organize an expansionist movement out of a previously fragmented tribal society, partly through an aggressive and demanding religion.

Arab warriors like these often used the tactic of the surprise attack, after which they retreated into the desert, where enemies had difficulty following.

. . . The previously feuding Arab tribes were channeled into a communal obligation to perform jihad, or holy war, not to convert believers, but to achieve the universal domination of Islam. All of this . . . created a series of armies that had considerable incentives to succeed.[32]

The third reason for the success of the Arab armies was the effectiveness of their traveling methods and battlefield tactics. At first, they had few horses and rode mainly camels. Usually, they traveled along the edges of deserts, terrain they knew well and from which they could launch surprise attacks. They also took along women and children, who both tended flocks of animals for food and cared for the wounded. After capturing many horses from the Persians and Byzantines, the Arabs began to form cavalry units. Yet their main battlefield units always remained infantry, who fought with bows, spears, and swords. A combination of fighting skill, effective leadership, and high morale made these fighters very feared.

After overrunning Spain, the Arabs attempted to move northward into France. But the Franks (early French), led by Charles Martel, stopped them at Tours (later Poitiers) by arranging their own infantry in a huge square that the invaders were unable to penetrate. According to a contemporary Arab chronicle:

> Near the river Owar [the Loire], the two great hosts of the two languages and the two creeds were set in array against each other. . . . [The Arabs] dashed fiercely . . . forward against the battalions of the Franks, who resisted manfully, and many fell dead on either side, until the going down of the sun. . . . [Eventually] all the [Arab] host fled before the enemy, and many died in the flight. [33]

THE MAGYARS MEET THEIR MATCH

Even after the defeat of the Arabs, Europe remained vulnerable to foreign invaders. In the late ninth century, still another Asian-based people, the Magyars, migrated westward from central Russia. By 900 or so, they

In this engraving King Otto I defeats the Magyars near Augsburg, France. This ended the Magyars' attempts to conquer Europe.

had begun raiding the regions around the Rhine River in Germany and the Rhone and Loire Rivers in France. And in 955, a force of nearly forty thousand Magyars (an unusually large army for the time) invaded the Frankish kingdom ruled by King Otto I.

The threat Otto faced was great. Most of the Magyar fighters were cavalrymen who, like the Huns, were top-notch horsemen. Their main weapon was a sturdy composite bow, but they also carried curved swords and short battle-axes, which they used after making contact with the enemy. They also wore shirts of light mail armor and leather helmets. In an odd but effective addition to Magyar defensive gear, the fighters braided their long hair into thick ponytails, two on each side, to protect against blows to the neck.

The most effective military device possessed by the Magyars was the stirrup. This invention had developed in the fifth or sixth century somewhere in central Asia and was later passed to the Magyars through contact with two other west Asian peoples, the Turks and Avars. Stirrups made it easier for riders to stay on their horses. They also allowed horsemen to start, stop, and turn more quickly and easily, which made cavalry formations more agile and deadly. A common Magyar tactic was to arrange the cavalry into a long line made up of several separate units. After these troops fired their arrows, some of the units would ride rapidly around the enemy's flanks in an attempt to surround them.

The Magyars also used the false retreat and other tactics that emphasized surprise and stealth. These were frequently success-

ful, until the fearsome horsemen met their match in the stubborn and resourceful Otto. The main Magyar force that entered France in 955 tried to besiege the city of Augsburg. But they failed because the invaders, like most Asian conquerors, were not proficient at siege warfare. As Otto's army approached, the Magyar leader, Bulcsu, divided his own forces into two groups, one of which met the Franks head-on. The second group secretly crossed a river to the south and tried to attack Otto from the rear. The plan failed, however, because the timing of the two Magyar armies was off. Otto was able to engage them one at a time and crushed each.

MONGOL GOALS AND MILITARY ORGANIZATION

Although the Huns, Arabs, and Magyars all achieved considerable military success, by far the greatest of all the Asian conquerors were the Mongols. The scattered Mongolian tribes first achieved effective unity about 1206 under an extremely talented and ambitious war leader who came to use the title Genghis Khan, or "Universal Ruler." The khan soon opted for aggressive expansion, partly to secure his borders with northern China, then ruled by the Chin dynasty. He also wanted his new kingdom to grow rich through plunder and control of crucial Asian trade routes. Finally, the khan believed he had a divine mission to conquer all the nations of the world. After capturing an enemy city, he told its inhabitants, "It is your leaders who have committed . . . crimes, and I am the punishment of God."[34]

Spurred on by this arrogant credo, in only seventy years Genghis Khan and his immediate successors managed to carve out a truly enormous empire. At its height in 1280, it stretched from Hungary in eastern Europe to Korea on the shores of the Pacific Ocean. The reasons for this unprecedented success had nothing to do with the Mongols' weapons, which remained low-tech bows, swords, axes, and lances. Instead, their keys to victory lay in superior organization, discipline, strategy, and tactics.

The organization of the Mongol army, for example, was highly logical and efficient, partly because it employed the decimal system—consisting of multiples of ten. "A ten thousand strong division was called a *tumen*," scholar James Chambers explains,

> each *tumen* was divided into ten regiments of a thousand men called *minghans*, each *minghan* contained ten squadrons of a hundred men called *jaguns* and each *jagun* was divided into ten troops of ten men called *arbans*. The ten men in each *arban* elected their own commander and the ten commanders of the *arbans* elected the commander of the *jagun*. Beyond that the commanders of the *minghans* and *tumens* were appointed by the khan himself and given the military rank of *noyan*. [35]

This breakdown not only made for ease and efficiency but also featured a strong hierarchy (ascending ladder) of well-trained officers. They were promoted for merit, rather than for prestige or family connections, and closely oversaw every aspect of military preparation and execution. The officers fre-

This fourteenth-century Chinese painting shows a Mongolian horse archer.

quently inspected weapons and supplies, for instance, and severely punished soldiers who shirked their duties.

Masters of Stealth Warfare

This system demanded and maintained strict discipline among the rank-and-file Mongol soldiers, who had already been toughened by physically hard lives as poor herders and hunters. And like the Huns and Magyars, Mongol warriors became expert riders. They "rode even before they could walk," Archer writes, "and learned to live on their horses for days on end, subsisting on dried meat, millet, yogurt, and koumiss (fermented mare's milk)." [36] Another example of Mongol toughness, as well as cleverness, was the manner in which warriors dealt with enemy arrows. Archer continues:

> All Mongol soldiers wore a long undershirt made of silk, which prevented arrows from penetrating too deeply [because of its strength] as well as permitting the soldier to withdraw the arrow from the wound by carefully drawing out the silk and untwisting it along the same path the arrow had originally taken.[37]

As for strategy and tactics, the Mongols elevated the techniques of indirect, stealth warfare—used in varying degrees by earlier Asian conquerors—to a high art. According to military historian John R. Elting:

> Chinese armies of infantry and chariots seldom caught up with them. When they did, the [Mongols'] normal strategy was to retreat slowly, luring the Chinese out into the wastelands where fatigue, hunger, and thirst would make them easy prey. . . . A favorite ruse was a feigned retreat to draw the enemy into broken or barren country where his forces would soon become disorganized and exhausted. Another variant was for the retreating Mongol army to lure its pursuers into a large-scale ambush set up by another Mongol army. A third

was for the Mongols to retreat so rapidly that the enemy would lose all contact with them; then, several days later, to change to their best horses and make a forced march back to catch their enemy off guard. If a surrounded enemy army stood and fought, an apparently safe line of retreat might be left open to lure it into a Mongol trap or simply to take advantage of the confusion of its retreat. A defeated enemy was pursued and slaughtered systematically; special efforts were made to hunt down the enemy commanders.[38]

Eventually, like the Huns, Arabs, and Magyars before them, the Mongols lost their initial momentum. By the end of the thirteenth century, the immense Mongol realm had splintered into four parts. At different rates, these steadily grew weaker and finally collapsed. Meanwhile, as had happened with the other Asian conquerors, many Mongols settled down in conquered lands and were absorbed into native populations. Because of these developments, the Mongols never penetrated Europe any farther than Hungary. Once more, the Europeans had been spared destruction at the hands of Eastern forces, and the West was free to continue its relentless march toward world military dominance.

Chapter 6
Musket and Bayonet: Linear Warfare Emerges

The transition from medieval warfare to early modern warfare began in the 1600s in Europe. The period from the Thirty Years' War (1618–1648) to the final defeat of French dictator and military innovator Napoleon Bonaparte in 1815 witnessed a series of crucial revolutions in military weapons and tactics. Handheld guns, especially the musket, advanced to the point where, supplemented by a new weapon, the bayonet, they dominated the field of battle. The musket-bayonet men marched to the field in columns, then deployed in long lines; because of the use of these lines, this kind of warfare is often referred to as linear. At the same time, muskets were increasingly supplemented by other firearms, particularly cannons, which steadily grew lighter and more mobile. Meanwhile, traditional cavalry units and tactics, as well as long, expensive sieges, began to decline in importance.

These and other military changes occurred against the backdrop of an emerging and grim reality of warfare in the European sphere. Many military historians call it "total war." It was characterized by long, relentless campaigns by large armies across immense territories; widespread looting, rape, and devastation of civilian populations; and the participation of many and diverse segments of society in war efforts.

Solving the Supply Problem

The first major early-modern demonstration of total war, coupled with new, more efficient techniques of waging war, was the Thirty Years' War. The conflict was caused mainly by deep-seated religious differences between Catholic and Protestant factions in Germany, which, at the time, was composed of many small independent states. It did not take long for Sweden, France, Denmark, and other major powers of the day to enter the fray. And, over time, armies ran amok, turning large sections of Germany and neighboring regions into virtual wastelands. At times, even the destruction wrought by the Huns and Mongols paled by comparison. The seemingly endless conflict, Christon Archer writes,

> destroyed libraries and archives, killed off productive segments of the populations, and severely damaged industrial and economic endeavors. There were many great battles, sieges, and

An eighteenth-century woodcut depicts one of the many massacres of civilians that took place during the Thirty Years' War.

thousands of now forgotten skirmishes between armed forces that ravaged or totally destroyed villages, castles, and towns. Peasants lost animals and seed, townspeople feared rape and looting by conquering armies, and in general civilians came to hate soldiers.[39]

Much of the destruction and mayhem stemmed from the fact that the armies involved were too large for the princes who raised them to pay or keep well supplied on a regular basis. So the soldiers paid and supplied themselves by looting and pillaging enemies and allies alike. According to military historian Archer Jones:

> Soldiers visiting a village often gorged themselves on the available food and stole the horses and much of the remaining food, including chickens, hogs, and cattle. They also looted the

houses, taking bed linen to make bags to carry booty and such items as a copper kettle, flattened to make it more portable. . . . Frequently they tortured civilians to compel them to reveal the location of hidden valuables.

The fortunate towns and villages were those that escaped destruction by making "contributions," essentially forced payments, directly to the military generals. Often, says Jones, "commanders raked off as much as a third of the payment."[40]

Seeing that logistics (organization, distribution, and maintenance of troops and war materials) was a mess, a German nobleman and military contractor named Albrecht von Wallenstein tackled the problem. At the behest of the leading Catholic leader, he raised an army and collected contributions from local cities and villages. Instead of pocketing the money, however, Wallenstein used it to pay the troops. He also gave strict orders that they must protect rather than harass civilians; that way, farmers could harvest their crops and merchants carry on trade unmolested, which helped ensure long-term supplies for soldiers and civilians alike. Wallenstein's efforts helped lead Europeans back to more efficient, sustainable state-run armies like those of ancient Greece and Rome.

Two of the leading figures of the Thirty Years' War: the Swedish king Gustavus Adolphus (left), and military logistics expert Albrecht von Wallenstein.

Tactical Advances

Other revolutionary military changes that occurred in the Thirty Years' War involved more efficient and deadly battlefield tactics, some of which placed increasing emphasis on muskets. The reforms of Swedish king Gustavus Adolphus, who involved himself early in the conflict, were particularly important. First, he devised new ways of breaking up and defeating the predominant infantry formation of the day. The formation consisted of several tight squares of pikemen, with six or more ranks of musketeers protected within the squares. Before Gustavus's reforms, Sweden's own infantry squares, like those of other states, did not fully exploit the offensive capabilities of existing muskets. At a given signal, some of the pikemen moved aside and the front rank of musketeers stepped forward and fired, after which that rank moved to the rear and the next rank came forward. The problem was that a single, small volley fired every one or two minutes was not enough to make much of a dent in an opposing hedge of pikemen.

Gustavus's solution was a mighty salvo of continuous fire by all of his gunmen. These soldiers lined up so that those in front were kneeling, those behind them stooping, and those in the rear ranks standing; then they all fired at once. This burst was enough to inflict considerable casualties on the opposing pikemen and temporarily halt their advance.

At this point, Gustavus sent in his cavalry. Most horse soldiers of the time rode to within a hundred feet of the enemy, fired their primitive pistols, and then retreated to a safe position to reload. Gustavus, however, had his cavalry fire their guns and then draw sabers (swords designed for slashing) and charge forward into the enemy ranks. Right behind the Swedish cavalry came Gustavus's own pikemen, who finished off or chased away any opposing troops that were left. The Swedes also introduced lighter, more mobile cannons for softening up enemy formations before the main attack.

More Advanced Muskets

The military tactics introduced by Gustavus and others in the early 1600s proved only a prelude to even greater changes in warfare. New advances in muskets, along with an effective new replacement for the battle pike, were just around the corner. The muskets wielded by Swedes and others in the Thirty Years' War were mainly old-style matchlocks, which used a match (smoldering piece of rope) to ignite the gunpowder lying in a small pan to fire the weapon. The process was time-consuming and inefficient, and resulted in frequent failed ignitions and misfires.

In the mid-to-late 1600s, however, the flintlock appeared. This more advanced musket used sparks from a piece of flint hitting against steel to ignite the powder. The gunmen poured the powder from a small, prepackaged paper cartridge, which also held the lead musket ball. (Each musketeer carried one or two dozen cartridges in a specially designed belt.) Though some misfires still occurred, the new process was more reliable and increased the speed of

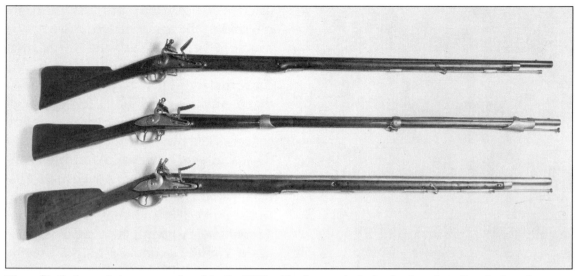

These flintlock muskets were produced in the 1700s. Used extensively in the American Revolution, they were a mainstay of early linear warfare.

loading the gun. "With a flintlock," Jones explains,

> the musketeer bit off the end of the cartridge with his teeth, retaining the ball in his mouth; used some powder from the cartridge to fill the pan and poured the remainder down the barrel, following it with the ball from his mouth and the paper of the cartridge; he then used his ramrod to drive the paper and ball down on the powder, and he was ready to fire. Instead of one round a minute [average for a matchlock], the soldier with a flintlock with paper cartridge could fire two or three or even more rounds in a minute. [41]

The flintlock's easier loading process also changed the composition of infantry formations. In the past, at least a yard was needed between musketeers to give them enough elbow room to load. With the flintlock, by comparison, each soldier needed less than two feet of space, which meant that a general could almost double the number of gunmen in each rank. This naturally increased the firepower of each rank as well. Flintlock muskets began to be manufactured in quantity in the 1690s, and the British, French, Dutch, and others standardized their own versions in the early 1700s.

THE BAYONET AND LINEAR WARFARE

Although flintlock muskets were the most reliable handheld guns yet devised, they were still not formidable enough to attack enemy pikemen or stop a large cavalry charge alone. Rows of pikes like those used by Gustavus Adolphus and others in the Thirty Years' War were still needed to protect the musketeers. However, military planners quickly realized that a single

A modern reenactor demonstrates a musket with a bayonet dating from the late 1700s.

weapon that combined the lethal qualities of both gun and pike would be more devastating than either. It would also be more efficient because it would eliminate the need to train and deploy two very different kinds of infantry simultaneously. To this end, the bayonet was born.

The first version of the bayonet used widely in battle, the plug bayonet, origi-

nated in France in the mid-1600s. The name referred to the act of inserting a wooden handle at the base of the blade into the front of the musket, thereby plugging it. This converted the gun into a pike-like weapon that could be used both for offensive charges and to repel incoming cavalry charges. The plug bayonet had a serious disadvantage, however. After it was inserted, the musket could not be fired. This meant that a soldier could alternate between musketeer and quasi-pikeman, but he could not be both at the same time. Once again, Western technology quickly met the challenge by introducing the socket bayonet in the late 1600s. The new device "employed a metal sleeve that slipped over the muzzle of the gun," military historian George C. Neumann explains.

> Since the blade was now offset from the bore [inside of the gun's barrel] . . . the musket could be loaded and fired while the bayonet remained in place. Versions of the new socket design were widely adopted by both the English and French armies just after 1700—although the "plug" continued in use for at least another decade. [42]

The introduction of linear warfare, with its line of musket-bayonet men, inevitably led military leaders and planners to phase out the old medieval pike. And battlefield tactics increasingly stressed the firepower of larger and larger numbers of muskets. "The proportion of pikemen thus declined," says Jones, "until it fell as low as one-fourth of the whole of the infantry. Combats . . . tended to become contests of light-infantry using their missile weapons

[guns] but arrayed in lines."[43] Such formations became standard for more than a century and were the mainstay of battles in Europe's Seven Years' War (1756–1763, whose North American portion was called the French and Indian War) and the American Revolution (1776–1783).

THE TECHNOLOGICAL ARMS RACE

The emergence of these effective new weapons and tactical formations caused rapid changes in military affairs both on and off the battlefield. First, the new linear formations of musket-bayonet men further reinforced the primacy of infantry on the Western battlefield, a trend that had begun with the Greeks and Romans. Over time,

Linear battle units prepare to engage in the battle of Hastenbeck during the Seven Years' War.

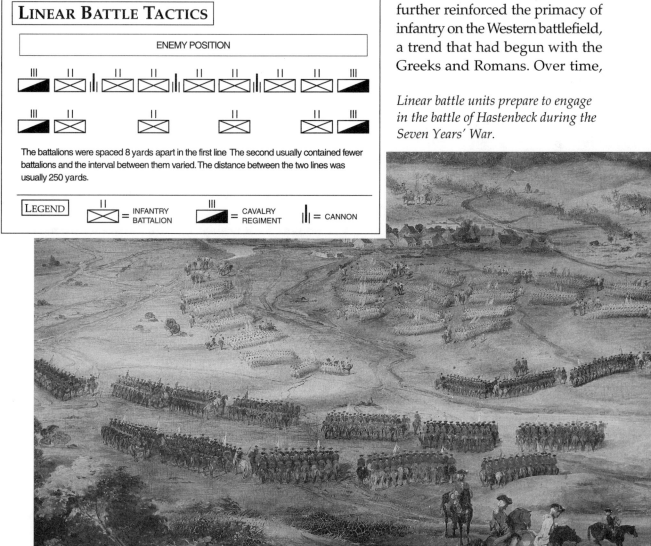

LINEAR BATTLE TACTICS

ENEMY POSITION

The battalions were spaced 8 yards apart in the first line The second usually contained fewer battalions and the interval between them varied. The distance between the two lines was usually 250 yards.

LEGEND   = INFANTRY BATTALION   = CAVALRY REGIMENT   = CANNON this had the natural effect of reducing the importance of cavalry. Simply put, the better and more lethal the firearms of the infantry were, the more vulnerable the unshielded bodies of horses and their riders were. By 1720, military scholar Martin van Creveld writes, cavalry "only constituted approximately one-third of the most advanced armies, and during the next hundred years this figure tended to decline until it was down to between one-quarter and one-sixth." [44]

Second, the relentless development of better muskets and other weapons further heightened the already brisk arms race among the leading European powers. Simply put, any nation that failed to keep up with the latest advances was leaving itself open to defeat, humiliation, and destruction. As Archer puts it, perhaps for the first time in history,

> the intrusion of technology in the field of military sciences compelled all nations, monarchs, city-states, religious leaders, and soldiers to accept the concepts of quite rapid change or progress. . . . The most successful nations were those that by one means or another adapted to [the latest] military developments. [45]

Two particularly lethal examples of this technological arms race involved field artillery. French, English, and Swiss improvements in the mid-to-late 1700s produced cannons that were even lighter and more maneuverable than those used by Gustavus Adolphus, yet with little or no appreciable loss of firepower. And the introduction of standardized parts and prepackaged rounds (like those of muskets,

only larger) almost doubled the rate of fire. Meanwhile, in 1784 English artilleryman Henry Shrapnel invented a new artillery shell that thereafter bore his name. It consisted of a hollow iron ball filled with small lead balls; when it exploded in the air, a deadly barrage of lead fragments showered the enemy.

NAPOLEON'S INNOVATIONS

These developments were followed by the last and most revolutionary series of changes in warfare in the early modern period—those of the French, especially under Napoleon. In 1792, shortly after the outbreak of the French Revolution, the revolutionary government passed a decree calling for the entire nation to mobilize for war. "All Frenchmen are permanently requisitioned for service," it read. "Young men will go forth to battle; married men will forge weapons and transport munitions; women will make tents and clothing." [46] This set a precedent that many large nations would follow in the future. "The nature of modern warfare had entered a new phase," in Archer's words, "one in which total effort was demanded of the populace regardless of age, gender, race, or creed." [47]

Thanks to the new, large-scale French levies, when Napoleon began leading France's armies in 1796, he was able to assemble truly enormous fighting forces. Between 1800 and 1812, French military rolls listed some 1.3 million men, and, at times, more than 200,000 of them were actively involved in a single campaign.

The Advantage of a Larger Army

Napoleon showed that having a larger army than an opponent can prove an overwhelming advantage if used properly, as explained by military historian Archer Jones in The Art of War in the Western World.

"If all men of two forces, equal in skill but unequal in size, could fire at one another, each combatant would suffer losses proportional to the quantity of bullets received. Thus, if force A had double the men of force B, B's would receive twice the bullets and have twice the casualties of A. . . . [As the battle progressed, A's advantage would continue to grow as B's force got smaller and smaller. Therefore,] when all men on both sides can fight with missiles, numerical superiority confers a disproportionate advantage. . . . In fact, under these conditions, the fighting strength of forces is in proportion to the square of their strength: A force of 2,000 men is 4 times as powerful as the force of 1,000."

The key to Napoleon's success was not simply larger armies, however; it was his application of linear warfare in bold new ways. To begin with, he almost always sought to throw his enemies off balance by striking them hard and fast and then staying constantly on the offensive to deprive them of rest and resupply. "Don't give the enemy time to regroup," he advocated,

> Intercept him in his movements; and rapidly move against the different forces you are able to isolate; plan your maneuvers so as to be able in every fight to throw your entire army against portions of his. In that way, with an army half the size of the enemy's, you will always be stronger than he is on the battlefield. [48]

Napoleon's mention of isolating and striking different enemy forces referred to another of his revolutionary tactical innovations: the division of his overall forces into several smaller field armies. These armies operated simultaneously over areas covering hundreds or even thousands of square miles. Meanwhile, he coordinated their movements as if they were one big connected army. In this way, the French were often able to strike at or capture an enemy's army, supply depots, farmlands, and other vital interests at the same time. This approach also put the enemy in a position in which he had to fight immediately, whether he was ready or not, or risk total defeat.

Another tactic Napoleon used was to advance his troops to the battlefield in columns twelve ranks deep. Some of the men detached and formed traditional lines of musket-bayonet men. The rest remained in their columns and either reinforced the lines when needed or marched, still in columns, into gaps in the enemy lines. Napoleon also frequently bypassed fortresses and fortified

The Challenge of Supplying French Troops

During the Napoleonic era, France fielded huge armies and, therefore, needed unprecedented amounts of supplies. In this excerpt from World History of Warfare, *Christon Archer details some of the extreme efforts to keep up with demands.*

"When war cut off the supply of saltpeter from Turkey and when scrapings from stables and latrines no longer met the national requirement, chemists devised a way of synthetically manufacturing this critical ingredient of gunpowder. The copper required for bronze cannons was found by requisitioning church bells. The need for iron likewise was met through 'nationalizing' wrought-iron fences and gates. Private blast furnaces as well as confiscated churches and chapels were converted into cannon foundries. . . . New networks of roads, canals, and bridges enhanced the movement of artillery and supplies to the point where eighteen days' stock of food became the norm for the army. Each soldier carried three days worth of food, the bread wagons of each company hauled a further six days' supply, and flour wagons of commissary were responsible for the remaining nine days' supply."

towns, reducing the importance of siege warfare. This allowed him to save precious resources and still achieve victory by defeating the enemy in the field.

All of these tactics were important precursors of those used in modern warfare. Although each was revolutionary in its own right, as van Creveld points out, "together their impact was even greater than the sum of their parts." In particular, the new tactics signaled the death knell of old-fashioned set-piece battles in which two armies met on one battlefield and produced a winner in a few short hours. "Increasingly during the nineteenth century," van Creveld continues, "battles were to last for days and then for weeks or months. They did not take place at or near individual places, but spread until they covered entire regions, countries, and even continents."[49] After Napoleon, only the addition of a new round of technological advances in weaponry was needed to make the mass slaughter known as modern warfare a reality.

Chapter

7 Industrializing the Battlefield: The First Modern Wars

In the years immediately following the Napoleonic Wars, the onrush of warfare technology slowed considerably in Europe. And, soon, the impetus for technical change switched to America, especially during the American Civil War. Fought between 1861 and 1865, it is often called the first modern war because it was the first to apply the latest fruits of the industrial revolution on a large scale.

It was certainly not the last war to do so. After the conflict, the Western arms race resumed with a vengeance, turning out an almost bewildering array of technical advances by the close of World War I. (This immense conflict, fought from 1914 to 1918, pitted Germany, Austria-Hungary, and Turkey against France, Britain, Russia, and eventually the United States.) Those roughly six decades witnessed the transition from muskets to machine guns and tanks, and from old-fashioned wooden sailing ships to huge ironclad battleships. This not only resulted in more casualties in wars but also placed more emphasis on the effectiveness of the weapons themselves rather than on the number of fighters. Indeed, part of what has defined modern warfare ever since is the ability of relatively small numbers of soldiers equipped with advanced weaponry to defeat much larger ones having more primitive weapons. As historian Paddy Griffith puts it:

> The apparent failure of attacking armies to defeat defending armies, even when there was a heavy numerical advantage in favor of the attack, has often been hailed as the dividing line between the warfare of the past and that of the present, the moment at which Napoleonic conditions ceased to apply and First World War conditions took over.[50]

RIFLES AND REPEATERS

The first important example of modern weaponry—the rifle—began to replace the traditional musket shortly before the outbreak of the Civil War. The term *rifle* comes from "rifling," which is a set of spiral grooves etched into the inside walls of the gun's barrel. (In contrast, the inside of a musket's barrel was smooth.) When a rifle fired, the projectile moved through the grooves, making an unusually tight fit, and exited the gun spinning, which resulted in a more accurate shot and provided greater range and velocity.

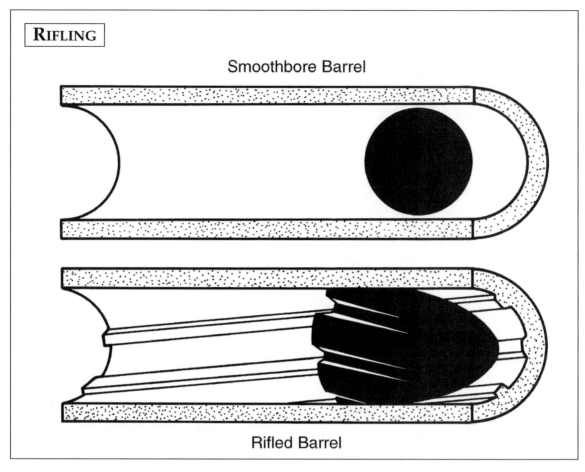

RIFLING

Smoothbore Barrel

Rifled Barrel

These were major advantages over the musket. Yet, for a number of years, the rifle was primarily used by only a few trained snipers and was not mass-produced for infantry. This was partly because the first rifles required more time to load than standard muskets did. Most riflemen could fire only about one shot per minute. In time, weapon designers overcame this problem, making rifles easier and faster to load.

Arms makers also introduced improvements that made rifles fire farther, more reliably, and more accurately. One of these advances was a small bullet that expanded in size after a rifle was fired so that it hugged

the grooves on the inside of the barrel even more tightly and flew more accurately after it exited the gun. The bullet was called the Minié, named after its inventor, French military officer Claude-Étienne Minié.

Better firing mechanisms also made shooting rifles more reliable. The first rifles used the same antiquated mechanism as muskets—the flintlock. Eventually, many rifles switched to the percussion cap, which consisted of a metal hammer attached to the gun and a metal plate, or "cap." The cap was coated with a chemical, potassium chlorate. And pulling the trigger caused the hammer to hit the cap, which flashed, igniting the gunpowder. What made the percussion mechanism so reliable was that the caps rarely failed to spark and fire the gun. Percussion guns were also simpler and cheaper to make than flintlocks.

Meanwhile, efforts were under way to make the firepower of rifles more formidable. It was clear to weapon designers that no matter how fast a soldier could reload and fire his rifle, he still could discharge only one bullet per reload. The solution was the revolutionary repeating rifle, or "repeater." It used cartridges containing multiple bullets, each of which entered the firing chamber automatically. The most sought-after and widely used repeating rifle of the Civil War was the Spencer repeater, named after Christopher M. Spencer, who invented it. The weapon could fire up to twenty rounds per minute, making its operator a fighter of unprecedented power and lethality.

MACHINE GUNS AND ARTILLERY

The success of the Spencer rifle and other similar repeaters immediately led to research into ways to make guns fire even more rapidly. The ultimate result was a class of firearms generally called machine guns. The first versions were primitive by today's standards, as they were cranked by hand and suffered from a heavy buildup of gunpowder residue that reduced their effectiveness.

A single-barreled, hand-cranked version, the Williams machine gun, invented

In spite of the increasing importance of the rifle, old-fashioned muskets, like these Confederate muskets, were widely used in the Civil War.

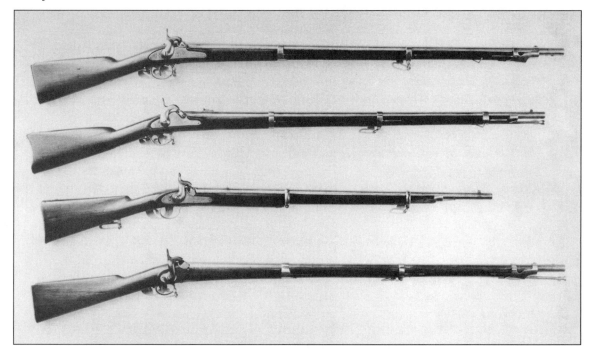

by a Confederate officer, saw widespread service in the Civil War. Another experimental machine gun of the era, the Gatling gun (invented by North Carolina's Richard J. Gatling), featured six separate barrels that rotated and fired in succession. The French followed up in the late 1860s with a machine gun with twenty-five barrels, which fired up to 150 rounds per minute. Yet in less than two decades this weapon had already become obsolete. In 1885, American inventor Hiram Maxim introduced the first easily portable, single-barrel machine gun, which fired an astonishing ten rounds per second. In 1889, the British army officially adopted the weapon, and the following year, the Germans, Italians, Russians, and others did the same.

Industrial innovations like those that revolutionized handheld guns also brought about major improvements in artillery. By the time of the Civil War, some cannons had become rifled, which increased their accuracy and range. Field artillery also became somewhat lighter and more mobile, and massed cannons were used against infantry with devastating effect in the American conflict. In July 1862, at Malvern Hill (in Virginia), a large Union artillery battery containing some 250 cannons mowed down several attacking waves of Confederate soldiers. More than five thousand men died, prompting Confederate general D.H. Hill's now-famous remark: "It was not war—it was murder."[51]

Following the Civil War, artillery technology accelerated rapidly. German weapon

A FAILED ATTACK ON FIELDWORKS

In the American Civil War and other subsequent conflicts that employed fieldworks (networks of trenches), the attackers often suffered horrendous casualties. A typical example was a series of Union charges against Confederate trenches at Cold Harbor, near Richmond, Virginia, in early June 1864. A Confederate officer, Colonel William Oates, later penned this riveting eyewitness account in his book, The War Between the Union and the Confederacy and Its Lost Opportunities.

"The enemy was within thirty steps. They halted and began to dodge, lie down, and recoil. The fire was terrific from my regiment. . . . They endured it but for one or two minutes, when they retreated, leaving the ground covered with their dead and dying. . . . After the lapse of about forty minutes another charge was made. . . . The charging column . . . received the most destructive fire I ever saw. They were subjected to a front and flank fire from the infantry, at short range. . . . In two minutes not a man of them was standing. All who were not shot down had lain down for protection. . . . The stench from the dead between our lines and theirs was sickening. . . . The dead covered more than five acres of ground about as thickly as they could be laid."

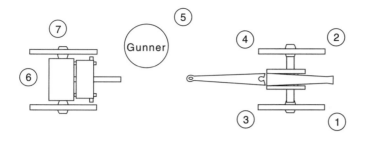

During firing, the eight-man artillery crew took their positions as shown in the diagram above. At the command "commence firing" the gunner ordered "load" and sighted the gun. #1 sponged the bore, #5 received a round from #7 at the limber and carried it to #2 who placed it in the bore. #1 rammed the round to the breech while #3 placed a thumb over the vent to prevent premature detonation of the charge. After gun was loaded #3 inserted a vent pick in the vent that punctured the cartridge bag. #4 attached a lanyard to a friction primer and inserted the primer in the vent. At the command "fire" #4 yanked the lanyard to fire. #6 cut fuses for exploding shells when needed.

The Four Basic Types of Ammunition

 SHOT: Cast iron with no explosive charge. Used against cavalry, troops in column formation, and buildings and other solid objects. Long-range.

 SHELL: Round, hollow projectile with a powder-filled cavity. Fused; exploded into 5–12 larger pieces. Long-range.

 SPHERICAL CASE: Hollow shell filled with powder and 40–80 musket balls that exploded in all directions. Fused; used at a range of 500–1,500 yards.

 CANISTER: A tin can containing 27–78 iron balls packed in sawdust. Can ripped open at the muzzle when fired. Range of 50–300 yards. Turned cannon into a giant shotgun.

designer Alfried Krupp introduced steel cannons that fired shells at an unprecedented rate of ten per minute to distances of up to three miles, five times farther than those used in the American conflict. Soon, smokeless powder was invented, which eliminated the smoke that had often obscured the sight lines of artillery gunners. Another advance was cannons with barrels that recoiled (sprang back) after each shot, making it unnecessary to reposition the weapons.

Needless to say, these advances filled many battlefields with devastating, deafening explosions that not only instilled fear in people but killed them. A German soldier caught in an artillery bombardment later recalled:

> We looked for cover, but where was one to find it in this kind of fire! The bombshells crashed through the clay walls as if through cardboard; and finally, raking fire set the village on fire. . . . Inside of ten seconds, four bomb shells and one shrapnel shell exploded right in front of us. . . . We all felt like we were in God's hand.[52]

TRENCH WARFARE

This wide and lethal array of firepower from rifles, machine guns, and artillery changed the face of warfare. Frontal assaults by infantry on positions fortified with such weapons became increasingly futile and fatal. This had the effect of forcing soldiers to seek cover, usually underground. As Christon Archer puts it, "Trench warfare emerged owing to man's natural inclination to dig in to avoid the deadly hail of iron and lead."[53] Trench warfare was used in the American Civil War, Russo-Japanese War (1904–1905), and on an even larger scale in World War I.

The average battlefield trench, or fieldwork, consisted of a ditch four to six feet deep with the excavated soil piled up in front as a protective barrier. Although protection for the defenders was indeed part of the strategy, there was also an offensive motive. Namely, when one side hid in a trench, it forced the enemy to approach on open, level ground in order to reach the defenders. This made the attackers sitting ducks, and heavy casualties were always the result. According to a German observer who watched British troops attack in waves against German positions in World War I:

> When the leading British line was within a hundred yards, the rattle of machine gun and rifle [fire] broke out. . . . Immediately afterwards a mass of shells from the German batteries in the rear tore through the air and burst among the advancing lines. Whole sections . . . crumbled under this hail of shells.[54]

To avoid such losses, the attackers often constructed their own fieldworks. Sometimes both sides periodically built new trenches still closer to the enemy, transforming a conflict from the traditional "offense vs. defense" mode into a contest between fieldwork engineers. This stalemate is sometimes referred to as "trench deadlock."

Such standoffs spurred a new race to develop even more lethal weapons that might break the deadlock by reducing the effectiveness of trenches as cover for infantry. One of these new weapons was the tank. The first tanks were armored versions of a recent agricultural invention—the Holt tractor. Weapon designers reasoned correctly that the tractor's revolving track, or tread, would allow it to operate on offroad terrain and to overrun trenches. In 1915, the British introduced the Landship tank, which carried two machine guns. The French also pioneered several early tanks, including one with a turret on top that revolved 360 degrees, allowing it to fire its machine guns in any direction.

Another weapon designed to counter trenches was poison gas. It was employed in small quantities by the Japanese in the Russo-Japanese War, but the Germans introduced it on a much larger scale in World War I. According to Martin van Creveld:

Employed under the right circumstances . . . gas was a very effective weapon since the same dugouts that

This photo of French soldiers standing in a trench was taken in 1916. Thousands of such fieldworks were dug in France during World War I.

offered protection from the shells were the first to be filled by the heavier-than-air noxious fumes. As a side benefit, not only did the gas kill and incapacitate soldiers, but it also frightened them almost out of their wits and forced them to wear cumbersome protective devices. [55]

Less effective against trenches were the first warplanes, which appeared in World War I. This was mainly because bomber planes were still very inaccurate. However, early warplanes carrying machine guns *were* effective in attacking troops caught in the open between trenches. Planes were also used to spy on enemy positions from above; to transport messages or drop leaflets; and to fly wounded soldiers away from the battlefield. The British built about 52,000 warplanes during the conflict, the French 51,000, the Germans 48,000, and the Americans 15,000.

One of the first tanks, the British Mark IV, *rolls over a low hill during World War I. Tanks were first built to overrun enemy trenches.*

BATTLESHIPS MORE POWERFUL BUT LESS FLEXIBLE

In this excerpt from Technology and War, *Martin van Creveld discusses the advantages and disadvantages of the new metal battleships built in the late 1800s and early 1900s.*

"Seen from a tactical point of view, each successive generation of battleships built after 1870 added speed, carried bigger guns, and had better armor protection, with the result that each was capable of blowing all its predecessors out of the water. Strategically, however, a navy made out of ironclads was rather less flexible, or at any rate more complicated to handle, than one composed of sailing men-of-war. Though successive improvements in engines permitted masts and rigging to be discarded, the endurance of coal-fueled vessels was always limited to a few weeks at most. For them to make really long voyages it was necessary to have bases, either neutral, friendly, or if possible wholly-owned. These bases had to contain not only coal but the specialized personnel, spare parts, and engineering facilities required for the resupply, maintenance, and repair of some of the largest and most complicated machines built by man. Tactical power was thus bought partly through the sacrifice of strategic freedom."

CAVALRY AND NAVAL WARFARE

While infantry weapons and counter-weapons were proliferating, the role of cavalry in warfare, at least in industrialized countries, was coming to an end. Most of the world's more powerful nations continued to fund cavalry corps following the Napoleonic Wars. But this was mainly the result of pigheaded reluctance to part with a time-honored, romantic, and cherished tradition stretching back into warfare's dim past. Large cavalry charges were still staged from time to time in the post-Napoleonic era. However, these always resulted in horrendous casualties and rarely had any decisive impact.

One exception was the effective use of horsemen in large-scale cavalry raids in the Civil War. The object in this case was not to attack infantry or other horsemen head-on but to disrupt the enemy's communications, supply lines, and way of life. Outside of these raids, however, mounted soldiers had no decisive effect on the conflict. In time, as cavalry "found itself confronted by increasingly deadly weapons," van Creveld states,

its functions more and more came to be restricted. . . . Though cavalry still had its supporters who went on prattling about the nobility of the horse and the magnetism of the charge, by 1920

The Confederate Virginia *and Union* Monitor *clash in the first battle between ironclad ships at Hampton Roads, Virginia, in 1862.*

its days on the battlefield were clearly over. [56]

Naval warfare, by contrast, significantly increased in importance and lethality as warships rapidly took advantage of new industrial materials and techniques. In the years immediately preceding the Civil War, old-fashioned sailing ships were already slowly being replaced by more maneuverable and reliable steam-powered vessels. At the same time, warships of this era were armed with much larger and more powerful cannons than those used in the Napoleonic Wars. These guns could also fire large explosive shells as well as old-fashioned cannonballs. The tremendous potential of such shells for the future of naval warfare became chillingly obvious in 1853, when six Russian warships fired such shells at a Turkish fleet during a battle in the Black Sea. In only a few hours, almost all of the wooden Turkish vessels burned and sank.

Naval engineers in Russia, Britain, France, and other countries began to realize that the threat of naval shells could only be effectively counteracted by abandoning wooden warships and building metal versions. Most were slow to implement such drastic change, however, until spurred to action by the use of metal-armored ships in the Civil War. In 1861, the Confederacy produced the first so-called ironclad by covering a wooden warship, the *Merrimack*, with more than eight hundred tons of iron plates. Renamed the *Virginia*, the vessel was severely tested in battle against the first Union ironclad, the *Monitor*. The fateful meeting took place near Hampton Roads, Virginia, in early 1862. For more than four hours, the world's first battle between metal-armored warships raged as thousands of people watched from nearby shores. Neither vessel was able to damage the other significantly, so the great duel ended more or less in a draw.

The showdown at Hampton Roads demonstrated to the world that the future of naval warfare belonged to armor-plated ships. The naval arms race that followed produced larger and larger metal warships, now called battleships. These averaged from ten thousand to fifteen thousand tons, about five times bigger than the largest old-style wooden warships. In 1905, Britain launched the HMS *Dreadnought*, a seventeen-thousand-ton battleship equipped with ten huge artillery guns. The vessel became the model other navies subsequently followed in building warships. By the advent of World War I, battleships featured guns that fired shells weighing close to two thousand pounds to distances of four or five miles.

Built in 1905, the British warship HMS Dreadnought *was the largest metal battleship of its day and was widely copied by other nations.*

After several decades of experimentation, another effective new naval weapon, the submarine, was perfected in 1914. The average submarine weighed a few hundred tons and carried about a dozen torpedoes. Most warships were able to avoid these underwater attackers fairly well, but merchant vessels were not; in 1916, German submarines alone sank more than 2.2 million tons of shipping.

THE TECHNOLOGY-ORIENTED BATTLEFIELD

The submarines, battleships, tanks, airplanes, and other advanced weapons built during World War I were significant in the overall evolution of warfare. As Archer points out, they

> marked the transition from a largely human-centered . . . to a more technology-oriented battlefield. No longer were moral qualities [of soldiers and na-

tions] sufficient to win. Now it was necessary as never before to integrate technology in the form of various weapon systems into the operations of war. Technology could more easily defeat technology, rather than relying on courage and discipline to overcome machine guns and artillery.[57]

More telling was the fact that those who fought this war, the largest in world history at that time, learned little about maintaining the peace that followed. Despite the conflict's terrible death toll of at least 13 million, no major moves were made to stop the escalating technological arms race. Indeed, the recent advances in weaponry only inspired more numerous and deadly ones. Meanwhile, the major loser, Germany, became obsessed with getting revenge on the victors. Seen in retrospect, this set the stage for the truly stupendous conflict known as World War II, which erupted barely a generation later.

8 Crushing Ordeal of Total Warfare: World War II

Among the many popular contemporary descriptions of World War I were the "Great War" and the "war to end all wars." These were certainly fitting for their time. But they soon lost their meaning and impact with the advent of World War II, which literally dwarfed the first global war. Lasting from 1939 to 1945, World War II was nothing less than a crushing ordeal of total warfare in which one side sought complete global domination and the other struggled to stop it. The aggressors were Germany, Japan, and Italy, known as the Axis countries. Opposing them were Britain, France, the Soviet Union, the United States, and several others, collectively called the Allies. Fighting occurred all over the world, but the two main regions, or theaters, of the conflict were Europe and the Pacific Ocean sphere. The sheer size of the war is reflected in two astonishing numbers. Some 70 million soldiers, sailors, and other combatants took part. And at least 45 million people lost their lives.

Not surprisingly, the weapons, strategies, tactics, supply problems, and other military aspects of the war marked the culmination of centuries of development and refinement. The combatants used every tool and method at their disposal and then invented new, even more devastating ones. These tools and methods, not to mention the actual battles and other events, were so numerous and complex that they defy brief description. However, a few snapshots of key weapons, tactics, and other elements of the conflict show its crucial importance in the long evolution of warfare.

INDUSTRIAL OUTPUT AND SUPPLY

The first snapshot of the war focuses on industrial output and logistics. Clearly, neither side could hope to win a truly global conflict involving millions of combatants unless it could produce and distribute massive amounts of food, clothing, weapons, ammunition, trucks, gasoline, and other vital war supplies. By the twentieth century, scholars George and Meredith Friedman point out, "Logistics had become, in effect, the tail wagging the dog." That is, armies in the field had become completely dependent on supplies and supply lines. The Friedmans continue:

> A Greek army could survive purely by forage if it stayed on the move. A division in the Franco-Prussian war of

In New Guinea, American soldiers unload supplies from ships for immediate transport to the front. American war production dwarfed that of Japan during World War II.

1870 consumed about 50 tons a day of food and fodder. In 1916, this number had risen to 150 tons . . . [and] by early World War II, about 300 tons a day were consumed in [operations in] North Africa . . . while Allied planners expected to spend 650 tons per day per division in France.[58]

In this respect, the Allies steadily outdid their Axis opponents. The Germans, led by dictator Adolf Hitler and his Nazi regime, began the war in a militarily strong position. Hoping to live off the supplies of their conquered enemies, however, they failed to establish a strong war economy. As a result, over time the British and Soviets manufactured twice as many tanks, guns, and planes as Germany did.

The Japanese also lacked an industrial base strong enough to wage a protracted global war. The Japanese islands had few natural resources, and almost all of the materials used in Japan's industries had to be imported. Some Japanese leaders recognized the seriousness of the problem. Isoroku Yamamoto, who commanded the Japanese navy at the onset of the war, warned his superiors that "anyone who has seen the auto factories and the oil fields in Texas knows that Japan lacks" the resources to wage a long war. "I guarantee to put up a tough fight for the first six months, but I have absolutely no confidence in what would happen if it went on for one or two years."[59]

Yamamoto's warning about the mammoth agricultural and industrial potential of the United States went unheeded. But his words were prophetic. After the Japanese bombed the American naval base at Pearl Harbor, Hawaii, in December 1941 and crippled the U.S. Pacific fleet, the United States began to mobilize. Only a year later, U.S. war production matched the entire industrial output of Japan, Germany, and Italy combined. And in the following three years, American workers built some 87,000 tanks, 296,000 planes, 2.4 million trucks, and 17 million rifles, in addition to thousands of ships. At the same time, American farmers produced hundreds of millions of tons of foodstuffs. As historian Louis L. Snyder puts it, "The Axis was literally engulfed under a sea of American war production."[60]

THE AMERICAN VICTORY AT MIDWAY

The Battle of Midway marked the first great turning point of the Pacific theater of World War II. The American commander and his officers received hearty congratulations from Americans of all walks of life and for good reason. It was the first decisive defeat the Japanese navy had suffered in 350 years. Japan lost more than 5,000 men, 4 aircraft carriers, several other ships, and 322 planes. The much smaller American losses were 307 men, 1 carrier (the *Yorktown*), and 147 planes. The decisive American victory did more than inflict heavy losses on the enemy, however. Forced to reshuffle their forces in the Pacific, the Japanese had to cancel their plans to invade Australia, New

Zealand, and other key Pacific targets. Moreover, the defeat of the Japanese fleet ended all threats to the U.S. west coast and put Japan on the defensive for the rest of the war.

American planes fly over burning Japanese ships at Midway.

CONVENTIONAL WEAPONS

The planes, tanks, and rifles mass-produced by the Americans and others, along with machine guns, battleships, and submarines, were the major conventional weapons used in the war. All of these categories of weapons had been used in World War I. However, most of the versions employed in the first years of World War II were more advanced. In particular, trucks, tanks, and planes were sturdier and faster; and their operators were equipped with radio equipment, which allowed them to receive and carry out orders more quickly and precisely. Moreover, each succeeding year of the conflict witnessed significant improvements in many weapon systems.

For firefights (exchanges of fire by infantry), machine guns and artillery were still the leading killers. Since World War I, machine guns had become lighter and fired more bullets per minute. The British used a reliable Czech-made model nicknamed the "Bren," while the Germans employed two models—the MG-34 and MG-42. The latter fired an amazing twelve hundred rounds a minute. American foot soldiers carried slower-firing but highly portable versions, including the M3 "Grease Gun" and M1A1 "Tommy Gun."

The Americans, British, Germans, and others also produced a wide array of artillery pieces. Some were designed to shoot down aircraft and others to destroy tanks, which were now more heavily armored than they had been in the first global conflict. The most effective and versatile artillery gun of the war was the German "88," employed against tanks, troops, towns, and aircraft alike. It fired fifteen to twenty

German 88-millimeter artillery guns ("88s") blast away at Allied planes. This weapon was the finest artillery piece produced during the war.

rounds per minute up to nine miles with considerable accuracy.

A much smaller antitank weapon developed in World War II was the portable rocket launcher. The American version was the M1, or "bazooka," which began to see service in 1943. The operator hefted the long, tubelike weapon onto his shoulder, and with the aid of a companion aimed and fired. Usually bazooka men tried to hit the sides of tanks, where the armor was thinnest.

THE ROLE OF AIRCRAFT

One weapon that really came into its own in World War II was the airplane. One of the first major indications that planes would prove far more deadly than in the past was the devastating Japanese attack on Pearl Harbor, almost exclusively carried out by combat aircraft. Two days later, on December 9, 1941, Japanese planes sank two British battleships, the *Prince of Wales* and *Repulse*, near Singapore. The second incident was especially telling because the ships were at sea and in full fighting mode (rather than docked like the American vessels).

The advancing speed and firepower of aircraft convinced the Americans that traditional naval strategy, which had been built around battleships, had become outdated. These massive vessels were now easy targets for dive-bombers. Moreover, battleships could not carry planes. The Americans therefore increased the strategic role of aircraft carriers, a gamble that paid off when they decisively defeated the Japanese in a huge duel of carriers and planes at Midway (near Hawaii) in June 1942. Thereafter, most

Three of the best fighter planes used in the war: the German Bf-109 (top), American F6F Hellcat (middle), and Japanese Zero.

large-scale naval strategy was centered around aircraft carriers.

The Japanese carriers that took part in the Pearl Harbor and Midway operations launched the most effective fighter plane

SATURATION BOMBING RAIDS

One of the most effective tactics used by the Allies in World War II was saturation bombing, in which huge squadrons of large bombers passed over a city and unleashed a rain of ruin. In the summer of 1943, for example, an Allied raid destroyed three-quarters of the German city of Hamburg. Leading Nazi Joseph Goebbels described some of the damage in this excerpt from his diary (quoted in William L. Shirer's The Rise and Fall of the Third Reich*).*

"July 26. During the night a heavy raid on Hamburg . . . with most serious consequences both for the civilian population and for armaments production. . . . It is a real catastrophe. . . . July 29. During the night we had the heaviest raid yet made on Hamburg . . . with 800 to 1,000 [Allied] bombers . . . a catastrophe the extent of which simply staggers the imagination. A city of a million inhabitants has been destroyed in a manner unparalleled in history. We are faced with problems that are almost impossible of solution. Food must be found for this population. . . . Shelter must be secured. The people must be evacuated as far [away from further danger] as possible. . . . Some 800,000 homeless people . . . are wandering up and down the streets not knowing what to do."

of the early Pacific theater—the Zero. Able to attain a speed of 330 miles per hour, the zero was the fastest attack plane in the world when it first appeared in 1940. Its firepower was also superior to that of any American planes in the war's early years. Meanwhile, in Europe, the German Bf-109 fighter plane was nearly the equal of the Zero at first and later, with steady improvements, surpassed it.

Eventually, the Americans surpassed both the Japanese and the Germans in both numbers and firepower of aircraft. In September 1943, the American F6F Hellcat fighter plane appeared. Faster and more maneuverable than a Zero and carrying six machine guns, the Hellcat was so effective that more than twelve thousand were in operation by 1945. For larger planes designed

primarily as bombers, the Americans developed the B-17 "Flying Fortress," which carried some seventeen thousand pounds of bombs, and the B-29 "Superfortress," with a payload of twenty thousand pounds. Fleets of these bombers pounded German and Japanese cities into heaps of rubble in the final years of the conflict.

TACTICS: OLD, NEW, AND DESPERATE

Overall, the strategy and tactics used in World War II were diverse and complex. The Napoleonic approach of attacking the enemy on many fronts simultaneously was applied on a huge scale, sometimes covering entire continents or seas. For example, in the space of a few days in December 1941 the Japanese attacked not only the American fleet at Pearl Harbor but also the Pacific islands of Guam and Wake and British bases all over Southeast Asia. The same approach was often used to capture a single country. In June 1940, for instance, Hitler ordered four separate German armies to penetrate France simultaneously at different points in the north and northeast. Soon afterward, his Italian allies invaded France from the south. In any such large-scale offensive, dozens and often hundreds of individual battles and skirmishes are fought.

Two overriding characteristics of the armies that carried out such offensives were speed and mobility (thanks to continuing advances in planes, tanks, and trucks, as well as radio). Thus, the conflict rarely got bogged down in trench warfare, a hallmark of World War I. Instead, commanders in World War II often opted for continuous movement, relentless drives into enemy territory, and, whenever possible, the element of surprise. The Germans took this approach to an extreme, especially in the early years of the conflict. They called it blitzkrieg, or "lightning war," which was designed to confuse and demoralize an opponent. "In a classic blitzkrieg attack," Christon Archer explains,

one hundred tanks followed closely by several thousand infantrymen on foot struck a front one mile wide, preferably by surprise.... Machine guns, artillery, and dive-bombers pinned the defenders down. Within a moment of coming into the open, the attackers were on top of their enemy, crushing defenses under their treads and shooting soldiers in

German tanks and troops sweep through the French countryside in a blitzkrieg, destroying farms and villages.

the back as they fled in panic. Tanks and motorized infantry then drove into the enemy's rear, up to one hundred miles per day, dicing armies like vegetables. [61]

Though extremely effective at first, the German blitzkriegs were eventually blunted by the increasing superiority of Allied armor, numbers, and strategic coordination.

The Germans, as well as the Japanese, also resorted to an older tactic that had been used in warfare for thousands of years—the massacre. The difference was that World War II witnessed the application of this approach on a scale never before seen; what had been an isolated terror tactic now became full-fledged genocide, the attempt to wipe out entire races and peoples. The Holocaust, the systematic murder of more than 6 million Jews by the Nazis, is well known and documented. But this atrocity was only the tip of the proverbial iceberg. The Nazis also murdered half a million Gypsies, 2 million Poles, more than 3 million Soviet war prisoners, and untold millions of Russian civilians, all in cold blood. Meanwhile, in the Pacific theater, the Japanese wiped out millions of Chinese and other fellow Asians.

The Japanese also used a tactic that appeared fanatical and irrational to Westerners, even to Japan's German allies. This was suicide, which was carried out either as an "honorable" alternative to surrender or to inflict disproportionate damage on the enemy. Believing that dying in battle guaranteed them a place in heaven, Japanese soldiers often charged in the open directly at Allied machine guns, forcing the defenders to kill them. Civilians sometimes chose the same path. In June 1944 on the Pacific island of Saipan, for example, American soldiers watched in horror as hundreds of Japanese civilians jumped off cliffs, cut each other's throats, or blew themselves up with hand grenades.

Not long afterward, desperate Japanese officers turned suicide into a formidable weapon. They created special units of pilots known as kamikazes (meaning "divine wind"), who purposely crashed their explosives-laden planes into American ships. In all, the kamikazes sank 34 vessels and damaged 288.

Secret Weapons and Codes

In addition to unconventional tactics, World War II featured several unconventional weapons and devices. Most were developed under a cloak of secrecy in order to surprise or maintain an advantage over the enemy. The British developed radar in 1939, for example, to provide early warning of approaching German warplanes. The radar worked by bouncing radio waves off moving objects and detecting the waves that bounced back on receivers, thereby revealing the locations and distances of the objects. The Germans developed radar, too, but theirs was much less accurate than British and American versions.

Most of the major combatants, Axis powers and Allies alike, also conducted research into biological weapons—the use of disease germs to kill people. The most active secret program was Japan's, code-named "Unit 731." By 1939, the Japanese had completed a germ warfare installation that employed more than three thousand scientists and technicians. It produced deadly cultures of typhus, cholera, bubonic plague, smallpox, and other illnesses. And tests were conducted on Chinese, American, and British prisoners, many of whom died horrible deaths. The Japanese also dropped fleas carrying bubonic plague on Chinese villages.

Meanwhile, the opposing armies maintained large units of code-making and code-breaking experts, called cryptologists. One of the most dramatic and decisive accomplishments of the war was the successful breaking of the Japanese secret military code by American cryptologists. They were able to read 15 percent of intercepted Japanese messages by April 1942 and an incredible 85 percent only one month later. On May 20, the Japanese inadvertently revealed the date and time of their impending attack on Hawaii, which proved a crucial factor in the subsequent American victory at Midway.

THE MOST DESTRUCTIVE WEAPON YET DEVISED

By far the biggest secret weapon of the war was the atomic bomb. The effort to build it—the Manhattan Project—was so secret, in fact, that the U.S. vice president, Harry S. Truman, knew nothing about it until he was sworn in as president in April 1945. A number of leading scientists had come to realize that splitting atoms of uranium and other radioactive elements would release unusually large amounts of energy, and that energy might be the basis of a weapon of unheard-of destructive power.

Worried that the Germans might develop such a weapon first, the U.S. and British governments launched the Manhattan Project

A mushroom cloud rises from Hiroshima only minutes after an atomic bomb leveled most of the city.

in 1940. After years of intensive development, project leaders tested the first atomic bomb on July 16, 1945, in the desert near Alamogordo, New Mexico. General Thomas R. Farrell, who watched from a bunker five miles away, later recalled:

> The effects could well be called . . . magnificent, beautiful, stupendous, and terrifying. . . . The whole country was

lighted . . . with an intensity many times that of the midday sun. . . . Thirty seconds after the explosion, came, first the air blast . . . followed almost immediately by the strong, sustained, awesome roar which warned of doomsday.[62]

Three weeks later, the Americans delivered the most destructive weapon yet devised onto a real target. The plane carrying the bomb, a B-29 christened the *Enola Gay*, reached the Japanese city of Hiroshima on August 6. At 8:15 A.M., the bomb was released and a few seconds later detonated at an altitude of eighteen hundred feet. The monstrous explosion obliterated four of the city's six square miles and instantly killed some seventy thousand people. Just two days later, another American plane dropped a second atomic bomb on Japan, this time destroying the city of Nagasaki. The Japanese soon surrendered, ending the war, rather than face the prospect of total annihilation. Caught up in the joy of victory or the despair of defeat, at the time few people appreciated that thereafter the entire world would be plagued by that same frightening prospect.

Technology Unleashed and the Future of Warfare

After World War II, technological advances in warfare continued to accelerate at an unprecedented rate, surpassing in only a few decades the accumulated progress of thousands of years. A few of these changes occurred during the Korean War (1950–1953) and Vietnam War (1954–1975). But most of the really radical advances came later, after the development of practical lasers, computers, and other revolutionary technological tools. Today, the arsenal of modern weaponry includes attack helicopters armed with missiles, warplanes invisible to radar, nuclear submarines, laser- and computer-guided bombs, satellites that sight targets and gather intelligence, goggles that allow soldiers to see in the dark, and many other high-tech devices that have changed the face of warfare.

Needless to say, developing this diverse and deadly arsenal has been costly. The twentieth century "ended with the most expensive arms race in history," states military historian James F. Dunnigan. "Between the late 1940s and the late 1980s, trillions of dollars were spent just on developing new weapons. This was more than was spent in any war in human history."[63]

The major portion of the arms race of those years was fueled by the so-called Cold War. This was the long political-military standoff between the two global superpowers that emerged from World War II— the United States and Soviet Union. In large part, the Cold War was driven by fears that one side might use its nuclear arsenal. In the years immediately following the great war, the Soviets acquired the atomic bomb; then both sides developed the even more powerful hydrogen bomb. The Americans and Soviets also built ballistic missiles capable of delivering these doomsday weapons to their targets with frightening speed. Although neither side resorted to the nuclear option during the Cold War, each felt the need to continue developing and improving conventional weapons.

The emergence of these two superpowers and their rivalry also sharply realigned the globe's traditional power centers. In the resulting new world order, Europe was largely marginalized (although the West remained strong thanks to the pivotal role played by the United States). "Europe ceased to be the center of world politics," Christon Archer writes, and nothing took its place. No longer did power on one continent determine power everywhere on Earth. Local power had to be struggled for in each region, and success in one region did not determine events in another. . . . These factors determined the nature of war and the role of force on Earth.[64]

Eventually, another huge realignment took place. In December 1991, the Soviet Union collapsed and broke up into nu-merous smaller states, leaving the United States as the world's only surviving su-perpower. Yet the end of the Cold War did not slow the pace of Western arms devel-opment, especially in the United States. Dunnigan explains:

> While the cause of it all, the Cold War, is over, the headlong plunge toward even more new military technology contin-ues. While the Soviet/Russian weapons budget has shrunk to a fraction of its

THE APACHE HELICOPTER

The AH-64 Apache helicopter is one of the U.S. Army's main high-tech antitank weapons and is also designed to provide air support for ground troops. When the troops approach an enemy position, the Apache flies in front of them. The pilot spots

the exact positions of enemy soldiers and then fires on them while the attacking troops move in for the kill. Looking some-thing like a giant wasp, the Apache is ca-pable of climbing 3,240 feet per minute and cruises parallel to the ground at 184 miles per hour. The Apache is equipped with some of the most advanced computer and laser systems available, including an infrared night-vision system allowing the pilot to fly safely at night at low altitudes. The helicopter also has a radar-warning device that tells the pilot when enemy radar has locked on to it. This allows the craft to use evasive maneuvers immedi-ately and escape attack by bullets and mis-siles.

A squadron of Apache helicopters, each a lethal killing machine, flies a mission.

The American M1A1 Abrams tank was the workhorse of both desert wars against Iraq.

Cold War size, American spending has declined much less. Other Western nations are also still spending at a large fraction of their Cold War levels.[65]

THE HIGH-TECH BATTLEFIELD

The fruits of such arms spending in the West were displayed for all to see during the American invasion of Iraq in 2003. Precision bombing of phenomenal accuracy, greatly superior mobility and firepower, and night-vision capabilities were among the key factors in the rapid and overwhelming American victory. Some of the weapons used in the war had seen action in the 1991 Persian Gulf War (in which a coalition led by the United States forced the Iraqis to give up the tiny country of Kuwait, which they had recently overrun).

But marked improvements had been made in many weapons systems in the twelve years separating the conflicts.

The workhorse, so to speak, of both of these desert wars was the M1A1 Abrams tank, which some military experts have called the finest, most powerful tank ever built. The newest version, which saw combat in Iraq in 2003, weighs sixty-seven tons. Even at this weight, its fifteen-hundred-horsepower gas turbine engine propels it and its four-man crew to a top speed of forty-two miles per hour. The M1A1 fires a special nonnuclear shell called a uranium bolt, which can travel up to two miles and easily penetrate the armor of conventional enemy tanks. The M1A1 also features sophisticated devices designed to protect the crew from nuclear, chemical, and biological attacks.

Also used extensively in both gulf wars was the Tomahawk cruise missile. A weapon of incredible accuracy, it is twenty feet long, can travel up to fifteen hundred miles, and carries a one-thousand-pound warhead, enough explosives to destroy a factory, bridge, or nearly any conventional military target. Cruise missiles launch from surface ships or submarines. As one approaches the shore, it flies near ground level to escape enemy radar and finds its target using a complex computer program.

Among the other advanced American weapon systems used in the Persian Gulf was the stealth bomber. These planes are covered with materials with odd geometric shapes that break up radio waves, making the planes hard or impossible to detect by radar. The high-tech battlefield also features another unusual American aircraft, the AWAC, which acts as an airborne command center for planes. Using sophisticated radar, an AWAC can monitor the positions of hundreds of enemy and friendly aircraft simultaneously and make sure that none are on a collision course.

Another high-tech system for location and monitoring utilizes satellites in orbit around Earth. It is called GPS, which stands for Global Positioning System. Signals from four satellites can simultaneously pinpoint the location of a person holding a receiver, which can be compact enough to fit in a pocket. GPS keeps combat units and individual soldiers from getting lost in unfamiliar territory, and it can also be used to guide bombs to their targets. In the 2003 conflict in Iraq, such "smart" bombs, called JDAMs (Joint Direct Attack Munitions), struck Iraqi targets with almost pinpoint accuracy. (Other kinds of smart bombs are laser guided.) And satellites now perform a wide array of other military functions, as George and Meredith Friedman explain:

> Satellites in space have both altitude and safety. They can see far more than aircraft, and unlike aircraft, they are exceedingly difficult to shoot down—at least for the time being. They can also carry out a wide range of functions, from . . . intercepting enemy signals and radar emissions to detecting rocket launches to relaying communications. Had these satellites not existed during the Gulf War or had they been destroyed, it is unlikely that war planners would have known the structure and weaknesses of the Iraqi air defense system. . . . Without infrared satellites, they could not have planned the air and ground campaign. And without communication satellites they could not have controlled and commanded a multidivisional force.[66]

THE UNCONVENTIONAL WARFARE OF TERRORISM

All of these high-tech weapon systems have proved extremely effective on the traditional battlefield, that is, when organized armies clash in an attempt to gain or defend territory. Such weapons are in varying degrees less effective, however, in a very different kind of warfare that has emerged in recent years: the covert (undercover), guerrilla style of fighting employed by terrorist groups. Terrorists are usually driven to violence by deep-seated, often extreme political or religious beliefs or by out-and-out hatred. Typically, they try to avoid open, one-on-one confrontation with trained soldiers and armies, opting instead for tactics such as assassination, sniping from hidden positions, and suicide bombings of both military and civilian targets. Because they work in secret and launch surprise attacks, they are unpredictable and extremely difficult to defend against by traditional military means.

So far, most successful terrorist groups have pursued their goals using low-tech weapons and tools such as ordinary guns, bombs, and aircraft. These can do considerable damage, as well as spread fear, however. The most dramatic example occurred on September 11, 2001, when a group of Islamic terrorists flew jetliners into the Twin Towers of New York's World Trade Center. The buildings were destroyed and about three thousand people lost their lives.

In response, the U.S. government, directed by President George W. Bush, declared war on terrorism. Government spokesmen,

Two JDAM "smart" bombs rest near a warplane on the deck of the USS Abraham Lincoln *during the American attack on Iraq.*

The second plane is about to strike the South Tower of the World Trade Center on September 11, 2001. The terrorist attack killed about three thousand people.

military experts, and media commentators all agree that this conflict is like no other before it. First, a single terrorist group can have members spread across the world, whenever possible living in secret in tiny groups. Traditional armies are useless against such a foe, and the most effective antiterrorist tactics involve spying and detective work. Second, the fight against terrorism could conceivably go on for decades or even be unending, as new disgruntled individuals continually join the terrorist ranks.

Finally, most experts worry that terrorists might eventually acquire biological, chemical, or nuclear weapons. This would give terrorists not only the ability to kill millions instead of thousands but also the clout to blackmail governments into meeting their demands. Terrorist attacks using weapons

of mass destruction might also be hard to counter. Unless the perpetrators were working directly for an established government, which is usually not the case, the country targeted by such an attack would find it difficult or impossible to retaliate in kind. For instance, if nuclear terrorists were to flee to a neutral country, their pursuers could not use a nuclear bomb against them without killing millions of innocent people. It remains uncertain, therefore, where the unconventional warfare associated with terrorism will lead in the years to come.

THE IMMEDIATE FUTURE OF WAR

The direction that more conventional, traditional warfare will take in the near future is somewhat more certain. To begin with, high-tech weapons and communication systems guided by lasers, computers, and satellites will make the battlefield increasingly automated. Robots will also become more and more prominent. In a sense, today's cruise missiles are robots designed to find and destroy distant enemy targets; as time goes on, other kinds of remotely guided robot weapons will attack by both land and sea as well as by air.

Computers will be used for much more than guidance, however. Some American soldiers, including pilots and tank crews, already supplement their training with virtual-reality computer displays that provide three-dimensional simulations of real battle conditions. In the future such training tools will become increasingly sophisticated and all soldiers will utilize them. At the same time, army-sponsored computer hackers will use advanced skills and programs to destroy an enemy's military computers. Computers, as well as other electronic equipment, will also be disabled by huge electronic pulses emitted by generators floating in Earth's orbit.

These advances in conventional arms, along with the spread of terrorist and antiterrorist tactics, suggest that violence and war will continue to be common ways to resolve human differences. It is worth noting, however, that recently, for the first time in history, public attitudes about the necessity of war have begun to change. Since 1945, Archer points out, as compared to the centuries that preceded World War II,

the power of the militaristic tradition has declined, and a liberal view, antimilitaristic . . . in tone, has achieved a limited victory in the Western world as

Soldiers use computers to monitor a training exercise in which tank units fight on an electronic battlefield. Such simulations are becoming more and more common.

THE END OF TOTAL WAR?

In the future, say George and Meredith Friedman in this excerpt from their book on the future of warfare, increased automation and accuracy in weaponry will reduce the large-scale devastation associated with the total warfare of World War II.

"Modern war became total war because of the inaccuracy of weapons. . . . The distinction between civilian and soldier was obliterated. Everyone fought or worked, and everything was at risk. War became a social catastrophe more than a political one. . . . With precision-guided munitions, the number of men involved in arms factories and armies will decline . . . [since] one projectile can be fired for every thousand previously needed. More important, the level of devastation will decline as well. The relatively light damage to Iraq in the six-week bombing campaign [in the 1991 Gulf War] . . . is a foretaste of a more moderate sort of war. More precisely, in seeing the end of total war, we see an end to an era where war puts society's very being at stake. Regimes may rise and fall, but as in the pre-modern era, the life of ordinary men will go on."

a whole. The public no longer regards war as good in itself, but at best as a necessary evil. . . . Western populations remain willing to defend themselves against aggression. . . . Still, to an unprecedented degree, sizable elements of Western populations have openly opposed the wars of their own countries while these were still being fought. . . . Many citizens have demanded the freedom to support or oppose a war depending on their own individual assessment of its justice.[67]

No one knows whether such antiwar attitudes will continue to spread or eventually dissipate and have little effect on the waging of war. What is certain is that, at least for the present and the foreseeable future, war will remain a reality of world affairs. Moreover, the West, led most forcefully by the world's lone superpower, the United States, will play the central role in shaping the nature of warfare. As the Friedmans put it in a powerfully worded statement:

Just as the gun shaped European power and culture, it appears . . . that precision-guided munitions will shape American power and culture. Just as Europe expanded war and its power to the global oceans, the United States is expanding war and its power into space. . . . Just as Europe shaped the world for half a millennium, so too the United States will shape the world for at least that length of time. For better or worse, America has seized hold of the future of war, and with it—for a time—the future of humanity.[68]

Notes

Introduction: The Most Theatrical of Human Activities

1. Victor D. Hanson, *The Soul of Battle.* New York: Free Press, 1999, p. 5.

2. Hanson, *Soul of Battle*, p. 5.

3. Lawrence H. Keeley, *War Before Civilization: The Myth of the Peaceful Savage.* New York: Oxford University Press, 1996, p. 3.

4. John Hackett, ed., *Warfare in the Ancient World.* New York: Facts On File, 1989, p. 7.

Chapter 1: Stone Age Warfare and the Native Americans

5. Arther Ferrill, *The Origins of War.* Boulder, CO: Westview, 1997, p. 20.

6. Tom Holm, "Warriors and Warfare," in Frederick E. Hoxie, ed., *Encyclopedia of North American Indians.* Boston: Houghton Mifflin, 1996, p. 667.

7. Keeley, *War Before Civilization*, p. 67.

8. Ferrill, *The Origins of War*, p. 11.

9. Grant Keddie, "The Atlatl Weapon," Royal British Columbia Museum, 1995. http://rbcm1.rbcm.gov.bc.ca/hhistory/atlatl/atlatl.html.

10. Ferrill, *The Origins of War*, p. 19.

11. Ferrill, *The Origins of War*, p. 25.

12. Colin F. Taylor, *Native American Weapons.* Norman: University of Oklahoma Press, 2001, p. 15.

13. Ferrill, *The Origins of War*, p. 28.

14. Trevor Watkins, "The Beginnings of Warfare," in Hackett, *Warfare in the Ancient World*, p. 16.

15. Ferrill, *The Origins of War*, p. 23.

Chapter 2: Military Innovations in the Ancient Near East

16. Ferrill, *The Origins of War*, p. 38.

17. Ferrill, *The Origins of War*, p. 53.

18. Watkins, "The Beginnings of Warfare," p. 28.

19. William Reid, *Arms Through the Ages.* New York: HarperCollins, 1982, p. 11.

20. D.J. Wiseman, "The Assyrians," in Hackett, *Warfare in the Ancient World*, p. 48.

Chapter 3: Greece and Rome at War: The Rise of the West

21. Victor D. Hanson, *The Wars of the Ancient Greeks and Their Invention of Western Military Culture.* London: Cassell, 1999, pp. 19–20, 22.

22. Polybius, *Histories*, published as *Polybius: The Rise of the Roman Empire*, trans. Ian Scott-Kilvert. New York: Penguin Books, 1979, p. 509.

23. Simon Anglim et al., *Fighting Techniques of the Ancient World, 3000 B.C.–A.D. 500: Equipment, Combat Skills, and Tactics.* New York: St. Martin's Press, 2002, p. 204.

Chapter 4: Knights and Castles in Medieval Europe and Japan

24. Christon I. Archer et al., *World History of Warfare.* Lincoln: University of Nebraska Press, 2002, p. 217.

25. Archer, *World History of Warfare*, p. 204.

26. Christopher Gravett, *Medieval Siege Warfare.* Oxford, England: Osprey, 2000, p. 3.

27. Edwin O. Reischauer, *The Japanese.* Cambridge, MA: Harvard University Press, 1977, p. 53.

28. Quoted in Archer, *World History of Warfare*, p. 205.

29. Quoted in Archer, *World History of Warfare*, pp. 208–209.

Chapter 5: The Fast, Fierce Armies of the Asian Conquerors

30. Ammianus Marcellinus, *History*, published as *The Later Roman Empire, A.D. 354–378*, trans. and ed. Walter Hamilton. New York: Penguin Books, 1986, p. 411.

31. Ammianus, *History*, p. 412.

32. Archer, *World History of Warfare*, p. 128.

33. Quoted in Leon Bernard and Theodore B. Hodges, eds., *Readings in European History*. New York: Macmillan, 1958, p. 85.

34. Quoted in James Chambers, *The Devil's Horsemen: The Mongol Invasion of Europe*. New York: Atheneum, 1979, p. 14.

35. Chambers, *The Devil's Horsemen*, p. 54.

36. Archer, *World History of Warfare*, p. 175.

37. Archer, *World History of Warfare*, p. 174.

38. John R. Elting, *The Super-Strategists: Great Captains, Theorists, and Fighting Men Who Have Shaped the History of Warfare*. New York: Scribner's, 1985, pp. 227–28, 233–34.

Chapter 6: Musket and Bayonet: Linear Warfare Emerges

39. Archer, *World History of Warfare*, p. 292.

40. Archer Jones, *The Art of War in the Western World*. New York: Oxford University Press, 1987, pp. 215, 216.

41. Jones, *The Art of War*, pp. 269–70.

42. George C. Neumann, *Swords and Blades of the American Revolution*. Harrisburg, PA: Stackpole, 1973, pp. 22–23.

43. Jones, *The Art of War*, p. 247.

44. Martin van Creveld, *Technology and War: From 2000 B.C. to the Present*. New York: Free Press, 1989, p. 95.

45. Archer, *World History of Warfare*, p. 218.

46. Quoted in Archer, *World History of Warfare*, p. 390.

47. Archer, *World History of Warfare*, p. 390.

48. Quoted in Elting, *Super-Strategists*, p. 147.

49. Van Creveld, *Technology and War*, p. 123.

Chapter 7: Industrializing the Battlefield: The First Modern Wars

50. Paddy Griffith, *Battle Tactics of the Civil War*. New Haven, CT: Yale University Press, 1989, p. 15.

51. Quoted in Thomas B. Buell, *Combat Leadership in the Civil War*. New York: Crown, 1997, p. 89.

52. Quoted in Archer, *World History of Warfare*, p. 422.

53. Archer, *World History of Warfare*, p. 415.

54. Quoted in Geoffrey Parker, ed., *Cambridge Illustrated History of Warfare*. New York: Cambridge University Press, 1995, pp. 279–80.

55. Van Creveld, *Technology and War*, p. 176.

56. Van Creveld, *Technology and War*, pp. 174–75.

57. Archer, *World History of Warfare*, p. 510.

Chapter 8: Crushing Ordeal of Total Warfare: World War II

58. George Friedman and Meredith Friedman, *The Future of War: Power, Technology, and American World Dominance in the Twenty-First Century*. New York: St. Martin's Griffin, 1996, p. 32.

59. Quoted in Archer, *World History of Warfare*, p. 512.

60. Louis L. Snyder, *The War: A Concise History, 1939–1945*. New York: Dell, 1960, p. 294.

61. Archer et al., *World History of Warfare*, p. 528.

62. Quoted in Snyder, *The War*, p. 596.

Epilogue: Technology Unleashed and the Future of Warfare

63. James F. Dunnigan, *Digital Soldiers: The Evolution of High-Tech Weaponry and Tomorrow's Brave New Battlefield.* New York: St. Martin's Press, 1996, p. 17.

64. Archer, *World History of Warfare*, p. 549.

65. Dunnigan, *Digital Soldiers*, p. 17.

66. Friedman and Friedman, *Future of War*, p. 303.

67. Archer, *World History of Warfare*, pp. 568–69.

68. Friedman and Friedman, *Future of War*, p. 420.

For Further Reading

Books

Cherese Cartlidge et al., *Life of a Nazi Soldier.* San Diego: Lucent Books, 2001. This well-written, informative volume explores the ranks of the German army during World War II.

Peter Connolly, *The Greek Armies.* Morristown, NJ: Silver Burdette, 1979. A fine, detailed study of Greek armor, weapons, and battle tactics, filled with colorful, accurate illustrations.

Will Fowler, *Ancient Weapons: The Story of Weaponry and Warfare Through the Ages.* New York: Lorenz Books, 1999. Beautifully illustrated with color drawings, this volume traces the history of various weapons used in ancient and medieval times.

Christopher Gravett, *Knight.* New York: Knopf, 1993. Explains medieval knights' armor, weapons, training, and battle tactics.

Allison Lassieur, *Before the Storm: American Indians Before the Europeans.* New York: Facts On File, 1998. An informative, fascinating examination of Indian life and customs on the eve of European colonization.

John E. Stanchak, *Visual Dictionary of the Civil War.* London: Dorling Kindersley, 2000. This book is handsomely illustrated and provides a good starting point for young people learning about the subject for the first time.

Theodore Taylor, *Air Raid—Pearl Harbor!: The Story of December 7, 1941.* New York: Harcourt Brace, 1991. A very well written overview of the attack on Pearl Harbor, aimed at junior high school readers.

Internet

Brooklyn College Classics Department, "Warfare 1" and "Warfare 2." http://dept home.brooklyn.cuny.edu/classics/dun kle/athnlife/warfare1.htm. An excellent brief overview of ancient Greek warfare. "Warfare 1" covers infantry and "Warfare 2," reached by a link, covers naval.

Gene Dannen, "Hiroshima, Nagasaki, and Nuclear Weapons," 2000. www.dannen. com/moreinfo.html. A very useful resource that links the reader to sites containing information on all aspects of nuclear warfare.

Chris Mill et al., "Medieval Warfare," 1998. www1.enloe.wake.k12.nc.us/enloe/ CandC/death/warfare.html. Has many links to information about weapons, knights, fortifications, and so on.

Nautical Brass On-Line, "Codebreaking and Secret Weapons in World War II." http:// home.earthlink.net/~nbrass1/enigma. htm. A detailed presentation of modern wartime codes and secret weapons, with a large bibliography for further research.

Works Consulted

Books

Christon I. Archer et al., *World History of Warfare*. Lincoln: University of Nebraska Press, 2002. A comprehensive, well-informed overview of warfare through the ages. Highly recommended.

Jeremy Black, *Warfare in the Eighteenth Century*. London: Cassell, 1999. A handy general overview of the weapons, tactics, and military advancements of the century.

Jack Coggins, *Arms and Equipment of the Civil War*. Garden City, NY: Doubleday, 1962. This book by one of the great Civil War buffs remains the most widely read general summary of the weapons used in the conflict.

James F. Dunnigan, *Digital Soldiers: The Evolution of High-Tech Weaponry and Tomorrow's Brave New Battlefield*. New York: St. Martin's Press, 1996. A very comprehensive, well-informed look at modern and developing weapons and tactics and how they will affect the future of war.

James F. Dunnigan and Albert A. Nofi, *Medieval Life and the Hundred Years War*. www.hyw.com/books/history/1_Help_C.htm. This is a 200,000-word electronic book published in 1997 on the Internet that is readily available to everyone. Contains a great deal of information about various aspects of medieval warfare.

Arther Ferrill, *The Origins of War*. Boulder, CO: Westview, 1997. An informative overview of weapons and warfare from the Stone Age to the era of Alexander the Great.

George Friedman and Meredith Friedman, *The Future of War: Power, Technology, and American World Dominance in the Twenty-First Century*. New York: St. Martin's Griffin, 1996. Focuses on the changing strategies of warfare in the twentieth century and how countries will fight wars in the foreseeable future.

Christopher Gravett, *Medieval Siege Warfare*. Oxford, England: Osprey, 2000. A very well written and beautifully illustrated overview of siege warfare in the Middle Ages.

Paddy Griffith, *Battle Tactics of the Civil War*. New Haven, CT: Yale University Press, 1989. A first-rate study of the tactics used in this famous American conflict.

John Hackett, ed., *Warfare in the Ancient World*. New York: Facts On File, 1989. A collection of long, detailed essays by world-class historians, each of whom tackles the military development and methods of a single ancient people or empire.

Victor D. Hanson, *The Wars of the Ancient Greeks and Their Invention of Western Military Culture*. London: Cassell, 1999. One of the better general synopses of ancient Greek warfare for the general reader.

Archer Jones, *The Art of War in the Western World*. New York: Oxford University Press, 1987. An excellent academic, though nonscholarly treatment of the history of Western warfare by a respected military historian.

Geoffrey Parker, ed., *Cambridge Illustrated History of Warfare*. New York: Cambridge

University Press, 1995. This general but useful overview covers primarily Western warfare.

Kurt Raaflaub and Nathan Rosenstein, eds., *War and Society in the Ancient and Medieval Worlds.* Cambridge, MA: Harvard University Press, 1999. An excellent collection of essays by noted historians, each summarizing the basic methods of warfare used by an ancient people.

William Reid, *Arms Through the Ages.* New York: HarperCollins, 1982. This huge, detailed volume provides an excellent overview of changing weapons systems over the centuries and is beautifully illustrated with hundreds of accurate, helpful drawings.

Louis L. Snyder, *The War: A Concise History, 1939–1945.* New York: Dell, 1960. A fast-paced, well-informed general overview of World War II, featuring numerous excerpts from primary documents collected from American and German sources.

Ronald H. Spector, *Eagle Against the Sun: The American War with Japan.* New York: Free Press, 1985. Perhaps the finest single-volume account of the Pacific theater of World War II available. Highly recommended.

Colin F. Taylor, *Native American Weapons.* Norman: University of Oklahoma Press, 2001. A fine, up-to-date, handsomely illustrated overview of the subject.

Other Important Sources: Primary Sources

Aeschylus, *The Persians,* in *Prometheus Bound, The Suppliants, Seven Against Thebes, The Persians.* Trans. Philip Vellacott. Baltimore: Penguin Books, 1961.

Ammianus Marcellinus, *History,* published as *The Later Roman Empire, A.D. 354–378.* Trans. and ed. Walter Hamilton. New York: Penguin Books, 1986.

Leon Bernard and Theodore B. Hodges, eds., *Readings in European History.* New York: Macmillan, 1958.

Jean Froissart, *The Chronicles of England, France, and Spain.* Trans. John Bourchier. Ed. G.C. Macaulay. New York: P.F. Collier and Son, 1910.

Donald Keene, ed., *Anthology of Japanese Literature from the Earliest Era to the Mid–Nineteenth Century.* New York: Grove, 1955.

Polybius, *Histories,* published as *Polybius: The Rise of the Roman Empire.* Trans. Ian Scott-Kilvert. New York: Penguin Books, 1979.

James B. Pritchard, ed., *Ancient Near Eastern Texts Relating to the Old Testament.* Princeton, NJ: Princeton University Press, 1969.

Modern Sources

Simon Anglim et al., *Fighting Techniques of the Ancient World, 3000 B.C.–A.D. 500: Equipment, Combat Skills, and Tactics.* New York: St. Martin's Press, 2002.

Norman Bancroft-Hunt, *Warriors: Warfare and the Native American Indian.* London: Salamander Books, 1995.

Patrick Brogan, *The Fighting Never Stopped: A Comprehensive Guide to World Conflict Since 1945.* New York: Vintage, 1990.

Thomas B. Buell, *Combat Leadership in the Civil War.* New York: Crown, 1997.

Lionel Casson, *The Ancient Mariners: Seafarers and Sea Fighters of the Mediterranean in Ancient Times.* Princeton, NJ: Princeton University Press, 1991.

James Chambers, *The Devil's Horsemen: The Mongol Invasion of Europe.* New York: Atheneum, 1979.

Peter Connolly, *Greece and Rome at War.* London: Greenhill Books, 1998.

Ian Drury and Tony Gibbons, *The Civil War Military Machine: Weapons and Tactics of the Union and Confederate Armed Forces.* New York: Smithmark, 1993.

John R. Elting, *The Super-Strategists: Great Captains, Theorists, and Fighting Men Who Have Shaped the History of Warfare.* New York: Scribner's, 1985.

Peter Farb, *Man's Rise to Civilization as Shown by the Indians of North America from Primeval Times to the Coming of the Industrial State.* New York: E.P. Dutton, 1968.

Arther Ferrill, *The Fall of the Roman Empire: The Military Explanation.* New York: Thames and Hudson, 1986.

James M. Hadden, *A Journal Kept in Canada and upon Burgoyne's Campaign in 1776 and 1777.* Albany, NY: Joel Munsell's Sons, 1884.

Victor D. Hanson, *The Soul of Battle.* New York: Free Press, 1999.

———, *The Western Way of War: Infantry Battle in Classical Greece.* New York: Oxford University Press, 1989.

Frederick E. Hoxie, ed., *Encyclopedia of North American Indians.* Boston: Houghton Mifflin, 1996.

Grant Keddie, "The Atlatl Weapon," Royal British Columbia Museum, 1995. http:// rbcm1.rbcm.gov.bc.ca/hhistory/atlatl/atlatl.html.

John Keegan, *A History of Warfare.* New York: Random House, 1993.

Lawrence H. Keeley, *War Before Civilization: The Myth of the Peaceful Savage.* New York: Oxford University Press, 1996.

William H. McNeill, *The Pursuit of Power: Technology, Armed Force, and Society Since A.D. 1000.* Chicago: University of Chicago Press, 1982.

Douglas Miller, *The Swiss at War: 1300–1500.* Oxford, England: Osprey, 1999.

George C. Neumann, *Swords and Blades of the American Revolution.* Harrisburg, PA: Stackpole, 1973.

William C. Oates, *The War Between the Union and the Confederacy and Its Lost Opportunities.* New York: Neale, 1905.

Edwin O. Reischauer, *The Japanese.* Cambridge, MA: Harvard University Press, 1977.

Ian Shaw, *Egyptian Warfare and Weapons.* Buckinghamshire, England: Shire, 1991.

William L. Shirer, *The Rise and Fall of the Third Reich: A History of Nazi Germany.* Greenwich, CT: Fawcett, 1960.

Martin van Creveld, *Technology and War: From 2000 B.C. to the Present.* New York: Free Press, 1989.

John Warry, *Warfare in the Classical World.* Norman: University of Oklahoma Press, 1995.

Yigael Yadin, *The Art of Warfare in Biblical Lands in the Light of Archaeological Study.* 2 vols. New York: McGraw-Hill, 1963.

Index

Picture Credits

Cover: © Peter Turnley/CORBIS

Nicholas Zubkov/AeroArt, International,Inc., 36

Art Resource, NY, 28, 57

© Archivo Iconografico,S.A./CORBIS, 11, 17, 21(both), 66(bottom)

© Bettmann/CORBIS, 32(bottom), 38, 46, 51, 52, 60, 71

© CORBIS, 76, 83, 85(middle), 93

© Christie's Images/CORBIS, 19

© Werner Foreman/CORBIS, 49

© Rob Howard/CORBIS, 96

© Gianni Dagli Orti/CORBIS, 12, 24

© Hulton-Deutsch Collection/CORBIS, 15

© Carl and Ann Purcell/CORBIS, 14

© Leif Skoogfors/CORBIS, 96

© Paul A. Souders/CORBIS, 43

© Matsumoto Toshi/CORBIS SYGMA, 47, 48

© ReutersNewMedia/CORBIS, 95

© Ron Watts/CORBIS, 64

Corel, 85(top,bottom), 92

Dover Publications, Inc., 40, 41

© Hulton Archive/Getty Images, 61(both), 63, 75, 78, 79, 82, 84, 87, 89

Chris Jouan, 32(top), 37

© Mary Evans Picture Library, 33, 35, 54, 55

Stock Montage, 25

About the Author

Historian and award-winning writer Don Nardo has published numerous books about warfare in various ages and cultures, among them studies of weapons, tactics, and battles in ancient Egypt, Greece, Rome, the Middle Ages, the American Revolution, World War II, and the Persian Gulf War. His acclaimed studies of ancient history and culture include *Life of a Roman Gladiator, Women of Ancient Rome, Roman Roads and Aqueducts, The Ancient Greeks, The Age of Pericles, Empires of Mesopotamia,* and *The Greenhaven Encyclopedia of Greek and Roman Mythology.* Mr. Nardo lives with his wife, Christine, in Massachusetts.